NIST Special Publication 800-128

Guide for Security-Focused Configuration Management of Information Systems

NIST

National Institute of Standards and Technology

U.S. Department of Commerce

Arnold Johnson
Kelley Dempsey
Ron Ross
Sarbari Gupta
Dennis Bailey

INFORMATION SECURITY

Computer Security Division
Information Technology Laboratory
National Institute of Standards and Technology
Gaithersburg, MD 20899-8930

August 2011

U.S. Department of Commerce
Gary Locke, Secretary

National Institute of Standards and Technology
Patrick D. Gallagher, Director

Reports on Computer Systems Technology

The Information Technology Laboratory (ITL) at the National Institute of Standards and Technology (NIST) promotes the U.S. economy and public welfare by providing technical leadership for the nation's measurement and standards infrastructure. ITL develops tests, test methods, reference data, proof of concept implementations, and technical analyses to advance the development and productive use of information technology. ITL's responsibilities include the development of management, administrative, technical, and physical standards and guidelines for the cost-effective security and privacy of other than national security-related information in federal information systems. The Special Publication 800-series reports on ITL's research, guidelines, and outreach efforts in information system security, and its collaborative activities with industry, government, and academic organizations.

Authority

This publication has been developed by NIST to further its statutory responsibilities under the Federal Information Security Management Act (FISMA), Public Law (P.L.) 107-347. NIST is responsible for developing information security standards and guidelines, including minimum requirements for federal information systems, but such standards and guidelines shall not apply to national security systems without the express approval of appropriate federal officials exercising policy authority over such systems. This guideline is consistent with the requirements of the Office of Management and Budget (OMB) Circular A-130, Section 8b(3), Securing Agency Information Systems, as analyzed in Circular A-130, Appendix IV: Analysis of Key Sections. Supplemental information is provided in Circular A-130, Appendix III.

NIST Special Publication 800-128, 88 pages

(August 2011)

National Institute of Standards and Technology
Attn: Computer Security Division, Information Technology Laboratory
100 Bureau Drive (Mail Stop 8930) Gaithersburg, MD 20899-8930
Electronic mail: sec-cert@nist.gov

Compliance with NIST Standards and Guidelines

In accordance with the provisions of FISMA,[1] the Secretary of Commerce shall, on the basis of standards and guidelines developed by NIST, prescribe standards and guidelines pertaining to federal information systems. The Secretary shall make standards compulsory and binding to the extent determined necessary by the Secretary to improve the efficiency of operation or security of federal information systems. Standards prescribed shall include information security standards that provide minimum information security requirements and are otherwise necessary to improve the security of federal information and information systems.

- Federal Information Processing Standards (FIPS) are approved by the Secretary of Commerce and issued by NIST in accordance with FISMA. FIPS are compulsory and binding for federal agencies.[2] FISMA requires that federal agencies comply with these standards, and therefore, agencies may not waive their use.

- Special Publications (SPs) are developed and issued by NIST as recommendations and guidance documents. For other than national security programs and systems, federal agencies must follow those NIST Special Publications mandated in a Federal Information Processing Standard. FIPS 200 mandates the use of Special Publication 800-53, as amended. In addition, OMB policies (including OMB Reporting Instructions for FISMA and Agency Privacy Management) state that for other than national security programs and systems, federal agencies must follow certain specific NIST Special Publications.[3]

- Other security-related publications, including interagency reports (NISTIRs) and ITL Bulletins, provide technical and other information about NIST's activities. These publications are mandatory only when specified by OMB.

- Compliance schedules for NIST security standards and guidelines are established by OMB in policies, directives, or memoranda (e.g., annual FISMA Reporting Guidance).

---

[1] The E-Government Act (P.L. 107-347) recognizes the importance of information security to the economic and national security interests of the United States. Title III of the E-Government Act, entitled the Federal Information Security Management Act (FISMA), emphasizes the need for organizations to develop, document, and implement an organization-wide program to provide security for the information systems that support its operations and assets.

[2] The term *agency* is used in this publication in lieu of the more general term *organization* only in those circumstances where its usage is directly related to other source documents such as federal legislation or policy.

[3] While federal agencies are required to follow certain specific NIST Special Publications in accordance with OMB policy, there is flexibility in how agencies apply the guidance. Federal agencies should apply the security concepts and principles articulated in the NIST Special Publications in accordance with and in the context of the agency's missions, business functions, and environment of operation. Consequently, the application of NIST guidance by federal agencies can result in different security solutions that are equally acceptable, compliant with the guidance, and meet the OMB definition of *adequate security* for federal information systems. Given the high priority of information sharing and transparency with the federal government, agencies should also consider reciprocity in developing their information security solutions. When assessing federal agency compliance with NIST Special Publications, Inspectors General, evaluators, auditors, and assessors should consider the intent of the security concepts and principles articulated within the specific guidance document and how the agency applied the guidance in the context of its mission/business responsibilities, operational environment, and unique organizational conditions.

Acknowledgments

The authors, Arnold Johnson, Kelley Dempsey, and Ron Ross of NIST, and Sarbari Gupta and Dennis Bailey of Electrosoft, wish to thank their colleagues Murugiah Souppaya, Karen Scarfone, John Banghart, David Waltermire, and Blair Heiserman of NIST who reviewed drafts of the document and provided insightful recommendations. A special note of thanks goes to Peggy Himes and Elizabeth Lennon for their superb technical editing and administrative support. We would also like to thank all those who responded to our call for public comments for lending their time and effort to make this a better document.

Table of Contents

CHAPTER ONE

INTRODUCTION

THE NEED FOR CONFIGURATION MANAGEMENT TO PROTECT INFORMATION AND INFORMATION SYSTEMS

An information system is composed of many components[4] that can be interconnected in a multitude of arrangements to meet a variety of business, mission, and information security needs. How these information system components are networked, configured, and managed is critical in providing adequate information security and supporting an organization's risk management process.

An information system is typically in a constant state of change in response to new, enhanced, corrected, or updated hardware and software capabilities, patches for correcting software flaws and other errors to existing components, new security threats, changing business functions, etc. Implementing information system changes almost always results in some adjustment to the system configuration. To ensure that the required adjustments to the system configuration do not adversely affect the security of the information system or the organization from operation of the information system, a well-defined configuration management process that integrates information security is needed.

Organizations apply configuration management (CM) for establishing baselines and for tracking, controlling, and managing many aspects of business development and operation (e.g., products, services, manufacturing, business processes, and information technology). Organizations with a robust and effective CM process need to consider information security implications with respect to the development and operation of information systems including hardware, software, applications, and documentation. Effective CM of information systems requires the integration of the management of secure configurations into the organizational CM process or processes. For this reason, this document assumes that information security is an integral part of an organization's overall CM process; however, the focus of this document is on implementation of the information system security aspects of CM, and as such the term *security-focused configuration management* (SecCM) is used to emphasize the concentration on information security. Though both IT business application functions and security-focused practices are expected to be integrated as a single process, *SecCM* in this context is defined as the management and control of configurations for information systems to enable security and facilitate the management of information security risk.

1.1 PURPOSE AND APPLICABILITY

Federal agencies are responsible for "including policies and procedures that ensure compliance with minimally acceptable system configuration requirements, as determined by the agency" within their information security program.[5] Managing system configurations is also a minimum security requirement identified in FIPS 200,[6] and NIST SP 800-53[7] defines security controls that support this requirement.

---

[4] Information system components include, for example, mainframes, workstations, servers (e.g., database, electronic mail, authentication, Web, proxy, file, domain name), network components (e.g., firewalls, routers, gateways, voice and data switches, wireless access points, network appliances, sensors), operating systems, middleware, and applications.

[5] Federal Information Security Management Act (P.L. 107-347, Title III), December 2002.

[6] National Institute of Standards and Technology Federal Information Processing Standards Publication 200, *Minimum Security Requirements for Federal Information and Information Systems,* March 2006.

In addition to general guidelines for ensuring that security considerations are integrated into the CM process, this publication provides guidelines for implementation of the Configuration Management family of security controls defined in NIST SP 800-53 (CM-1 through CM-9). This publication also includes guidelines for NIST SP 800-53 security controls related to managing the configuration of the information system architecture and associated components for secure processing, storing, and transmitting of information. Configuration management is an important process for establishing and maintaining secure information system configurations, and provides important support for managing security risks in information systems.

The guidelines in this publication are applicable to all federal information systems other than those systems designated as national security systems as defined in 44 U.S.C., Section 3542. The guidelines have been broadly developed from a technical perspective to complement similar guidelines for national security systems and may be used for such systems with the approval of appropriate federal officials exercising policy authority over such systems. State, local, and tribal governments, as well as private sector organizations are encouraged to consider using these guidelines, as appropriate.

This publication is intended to provide guidelines for organizations responsible for managing and administrating the security of federal information systems and associated environments of operation. For organizations responsible for the security of information processed, stored, and transmitted by external or service-oriented environments (e.g., cloud service providers), the configuration management concepts and principles presented here can aid organizations in establishing assurance requirements for suppliers providing external information technology services.

1.2   TARGET AUDIENCE

This publication is intended to serve a diverse audience of information system and information security professionals including:

- Individuals with information system and information security management and oversight responsibilities (e.g., chief information officers, senior agency information security officers, and authorizing officials);

- Individuals with information system development responsibilities (e.g., program and project managers, mission/application owners, system designers, system and application programmers);

- Individuals with information security implementation and operational responsibilities (e.g., information system owners, information owners, information system administrators, information system security officers); and

- Individuals with information system and information security assessment and monitoring responsibilities (e.g., auditors, Inspectors General, assessors/assessment teams).

Commercial companies producing information technology products and systems, creating information security-related technologies, and providing information security services can also benefit from the information in this publication.

---

[7] National Institute of Standards and Technology Special Publication 800-53, *Recommended Security Controls for Federal Information Systems and Organizations*, as amended.

1.3   RELATIONSHIP TO OTHER SECURITY PUBLICATIONS

Configuration management concepts and principles described in this publication provide supporting information for NIST SP 800-53, *Recommended Security Controls for Federal Information Systems and Organizations*, as amended. This publication also provides important supporting information for the Implement Step (Step 3), Assess Step (Step 4), and the Monitor Step (Step 6) of the Risk Management Framework (RMF) that is discussed in NIST SP 800-37, *Guide for Applying the Risk Management Framework to Federal Information Systems: A Security Life Cycle Approach*, as amended. More specific guidelines on the implementation of the Monitor step of the RMF is provided in Draft NIST SP 800-137, *Information Security Continuous Monitoring for Federal Information Systems and Organizations*. The purpose of the Monitor step in the Risk Management Framework is to continuously monitor the effectiveness of all security controls selected, implemented, and authorized for protecting organizational information and information systems, which includes the Configuration Management security controls identified in SP 800-53. The monitoring phase identified in the security-focused configuration management (SecCM) process defined later in this document supports the RMF Monitoring phase by providing specific activities associated with the monitoring of the information system structural architecture and the configuration settings of the software and hardware that operate in that system architecture.

Many of the SecCM concepts and principles described in this publication draw upon the underlying principles established for managing information security risk in NIST SP 800-39, *Managing Information Security Risk: Organization, Mission, and Information System View*.

This publication often refers to information from NIST SP 800-70, *National Checklist Program for IT Products--Guidelines for Checklist Users and Developers*, as amended; NIST SP 800-117, *Guide to Adopting and Using the Security Content Automation Protocol (SCAP)*; and NIST SP 800-126, *The Technical Specification for the Security Content Automation Protocol (SCAP), Version 1.2*, as a potential means of automated support in conducting many configuration management activities.

Additionally, this publication refers to numerous NIST Special Publications that provide guidelines on use and configuration of specific technologies for securing information systems. Many of these publications are identified in Appendix F, Best Practices for Establishing Secure Configurations.

1.4   ORGANIZATION OF THIS SPECIAL PUBLICATION

The remainder of this special publication is organized as follows:

- **Chapter Two** describes the fundamental concepts associated with SecCM including: (i) an overview of general configuration management terms and concepts, and its relationship to security-focused configuration management of information technology (IT) and information systems; (ii) the major phases of SecCM; (iii) the fundamental concepts relevant to the practice of SecCM; and (iv) the primary roles and responsibilities relevant to SecCM.

- **Chapter Three** describes the process of applying SecCM practices to information systems within an organization including: (i) planning SecCM activities for the organization; (ii) identifying and implementing secure configurations; (iii) controlling configuration changes to information systems; (iv) monitoring the configuration of information systems to ensure that configurations are not inadvertently altered from the approved baseline; and (v) the use of standardized Security Content Automation Protocol (SCAP) protocols for supporting automated tools in verifying information system configurations.

- **Supporting appendices** provide more detailed SecCM information including: (A) general references; (B) glossary of terms and definitions; (C) acronyms; (D) sample SecCM plan outline; (E) sample configuration change request template; (F) best practices for establishing secure configurations in information systems, (G) flow charts for various SecCM processes and activities, and (H) sample Configuration Control Board (CCB) charter.

CHAPTER TWO

THE FUNDAMENTALS

BASIC CONCEPTS OF SECURITY CONFIGURATION MANAGEMENT

This chapter presents the fundamentals of security-focused configuration management (SecCM) including: (i) an overview of basic configuration management terms and concepts, and the role of SecCM; (ii) the primary phases of SecCM; (iii) SecCM concepts; and (iv) the roles and responsibilities relevant to SecCM.

2.1 OVERVIEW

This section provides an overview of SecCM including its importance in managing organizational risks from information systems, the basic terms associated with configuration management, and characterization of SecCM within the configuration management discipline.

2.1.1 BASIC CONFIGURATION MANAGEMENT

Configuration management has been applied to a broad range of products and systems in subject areas such as automobiles, pharmaceuticals, and information systems. Some basic terms associated with the configuration management discipline are briefly explained below.

Configuration Management (CM) comprises a collection of activities focused on establishing and maintaining the integrity of products and systems, through control of the processes for initializing, changing, and monitoring the configurations of those products and systems.

A *Configuration Item (CI)* is an identifiable part of a system (e.g., hardware, software, firmware, documentation, or a combination thereof) that is a discrete target of configuration control processes.

A *Baseline Configuration* is a set of specifications for a system, or CI within a system, that has been formally reviewed and agreed on at a given point in time, and which can be changed only through change control procedures. The baseline configuration is used as a basis for future builds, releases, and/or changes.

A *Configuration Management Plan* (CM Plan) is a comprehensive description of the roles, responsibilities, policies, and procedures that apply when managing the configuration of products and systems. The basic parts of a CM Plan include:

- *Configuration Control Board (CCB)* – Establishment of and charter for a group of qualified people with responsibility for the process of controlling and approving changes throughout the development and operational lifecycle of products and systems; may also be referred to as a change control board;

- Configuration Item *Identification* – methodology for selecting and naming configuration items that need to be placed under CM;

- Configuration *Change Control* – process for managing updates to the baseline configurations for the configuration items; and

- Configuration *Monitoring* – process for assessing or testing the level of compliance with the established baseline configuration and mechanisms for reporting on the configuration status of items placed under CM.

This guideline is associated with the application of security-focused configuration management practices as they apply to information systems. The configuration of an information system is a representation of the system's components, how each component is configured, and how the components are connected or arranged to implement the information system. The possible conditions in which an information system or system component can be arranged affect the security posture of the information system. The activities involved in managing the configuration of an information system include development of a configuration management plan, establishment of a configuration control board, development of a methodology for configuration item identification, establishment of the baseline configuration, development of a configuration change control process, and development of a process for configuration monitoring and reporting.

2.1.2 THE CHALLENGE OF PROTECTING INFORMATION AND MANAGING RISK

As the ubiquity of information technology increases the dependence on information systems, organizations are faced with an increase in the number and severity of threats that can have adverse impacts on operations, assets, and individuals. Given the potential for harm that can arise from environmental disruptions, human errors, and purposeful attacks by hostile entities and other threats, an organization must place greater emphasis on the management of risk associated with information systems as it attempts to carry out its mission and business processes. The cornerstone of any effort to manage organizational risk related to information systems is an effective information security[8] program.

It is incumbent upon the organization to implement its directives in a manner that provides adequate security[9] for protecting information and information systems. As threats continue to evolve in an environment where organizations have finite resources with which to protect themselves, security has become a risk-based activity where the operational and economic costs of ensuring that a particular threat does not exploit a vulnerability are balanced against the needs of the organization's mission and business processes. In a world of limited resources, the practice of risk management is fundamental to an information security program.

In risk-based mission protection strategies, organizations explicitly identify and respond to risks associated with the use of information systems in carrying out missions and business processes. Careful consideration is given to how a range of diverse threats can expose existing vulnerabilities and cause harm to the organization. In the management of risk, organizations often have very little control over threats. Organizations cannot control earthquakes, floods, disgruntled employees, hackers, and other threats; however, organizations can control vulnerabilities and reduce threats via implementation of a robust SecCM process that is part of the overall risk management process. Vulnerabilities[10] represent the various types of weaknesses that can be exploited by a threat. While an analysis of information system vulnerabilities reveals a variety of

---

[8] Information security is the protection of information and information systems from unauthorized access, use, disclosure, disruption, modification, or destruction in order to provide confidentiality, integrity, and availability [44 U.S.C., Sec. 3542]. For the purposes of this publication, "security" is used synonymously with "information security."

[9] Adequate security is security commensurate with the risk and the magnitude of harm resulting from the loss, misuse, or unauthorized access to or modification of information.

[10] A vulnerability is a weakness in an information system, system security procedures, internal controls, or implementation that could be exploited or triggered by a threat source [CNSS Inst. 4009, Adapted].

potential causes, many vulnerabilities can be traced to software flaws and misconfigurations of information system components.

The management of configurations has traditionally been viewed as an IT management best practice.[11] Using SecCM to gain greater control over and ensure the integrity of IT resources facilitates asset management, improves incident response, help desk, disaster recovery and problem solving, aids in software development and release management, enables greater automation of processes, and supports compliance with policies and preparation for audits.

2.1.3   ROLE OF SECURITY-FOCUSED CONFIGURATION MANAGEMENT[12]

The configuration of an information system and its components has a direct impact on the security posture of the system. How those configurations are established and maintained requires a disciplined approach for providing adequate security. Changes to the configuration of an information system are often needed to stay up to date with changing business functions and services, and information security needs. These changes can adversely impact the previously established security posture; therefore, effective configuration management is vital to the establishment and maintenance of security of information and the information system. The security-focused configuration management process is critical to maintaining a secure state under normal operations, contingency recovery operations, and reconstitution to normal operations.

Security-Focused Configuration Management (SecCM) is the management and control of secure configurations for an information system to enable security and facilitate the management of risk. SecCM builds on the general concepts, processes, and activities of configuration management by attention on the implementation and maintenance of the established security requirements of the organization and information systems.

Information security configuration management requirements are integrated into (or complement) existing organizational configuration management processes (e.g., business functions, applications, products) and information systems. SecCM activities include:

* identification and recording of configurations that impact the security posture of the information system and the organization;
* the consideration of security risks in approving the initial configuration;
* the analysis of security implications of changes to the information system configuration; and
* documentation of the approved/implemented changes.

In cases where an organization has no existing CM process in place, security-focused configuration management practices as defined in this document are developed and implemented from process inception.

---

[11] Best practices are often considered to be proven practices or processes that have been successfully used by multiple organizations. IT management best practices, as referred to in this publication, are viewed from an organization-wide perspective as practices that best support the mission and business functions or services of the organization.

[12] There are a number of organizations that have documented best practice standards and guidelines for configuration management which precede this Special Publication and influence its direction including: International Organization for Standardization (ISO) ISO 10007:2003; IEEE Standard 828-2005; the Capability Maturity Model Integration (CMMI) with their focus on configuration management for software development documents (http://www.sei.cmu.edu/cmmi/); the Information Technology Infrastructure Library (ITIL) for its influence on the integration of configuration within information technology management (http://www.itil-officialsite.com/home/home.asp); and the International Organization for Standardization (ISO) for its attention to configuration management within quality management systems.

Initial implementation of a SecCM program may require considerable effort. If there is no existing SecCM process within the organization, there will be an initial investment in developing and implementing a program that is comprehensive enough to span multiple technologies, the organizational structure, and disparate processes, and that can deliver consistent results while supporting the organization's missions and business processes. In addition, tools are procured and implemented, system components inventoried and recorded, and processes modified to account for new ways of managing technology in the context of SecCM.

Once in place, SecCM requires an ongoing investment in time and resources. Product patches, fixes, and updates require time for security impact analysis even as threats and vulnerabilities continue to exist. As changes to information systems are made, baseline configurations are updated, specific configuration settings confirmed, and configuration items tracked, verified, and reported. SecCM is a continuous activity that, once incorporated into IT management processes, touches all stages of the system development life cycle (SDLC). Organizations that implement SecCM throughout the SDLC and make its tenets a part of the IT management culture are most likely to reap benefits in terms of improvement of security and functionality, and more effective management of organizational risk.

2.2   THE PHASES OF SECURITY-FOCUSED CONFIGURATION MANAGEMENT

Security-focused configuration management of information systems involves a set of activities that can be organized into four major phases – Planning, Identifying and Implementing Configurations, Controlling Configuration Changes, and Monitoring. It is through these phases that SecCM not only supports security for an information system and its components, but also supports the management of organizational risk. Chapter 3 presents the detailed processes and considerations in implementing the necessary activities in each of these phases.

The four phases of SecCM are illustrated in Figure 2-1 and described below.

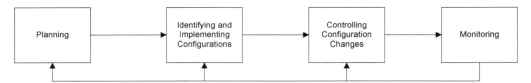

Figure 2-1 – Security-focused Configuration Management Phases

2.2.1   PLANNING

As with many security activities, planning can greatly impact the success or failure of the effort. As a part of planning, the scope or applicability of SecCM processes are identified.

Planning includes developing policy and procedures to incorporate SecCM into existing information technology and security programs, and then disseminating the policy throughout the organization. Policy addresses areas such as the implementation of SecCM plans, integration into existing security program plans, Configuration Control Boards (CCBs), configuration change control processes, tools and technology, the use of common secure configurations[13] and baseline configurations, monitoring, and metrics for compliance with established SecCM policy and procedures. It is typically more cost-effective to develop and implement a SecCM plan, policies, procedures, and associated SecCM tools at the organizational level.

2.2.2 IDENTIFYING AND IMPLEMENTING CONFIGURATIONS

After the planning and preparation activities are completed, a secure baseline configuration for the information system is developed, reviewed, approved, and implemented. The approved baseline configuration for an information system and associated components represents the most secure state consistent with operational requirements and constraints. For a typical information system, the secure baseline may address configuration settings, software loads, patch levels, how the information system is physically or logically arranged, how various security controls are implemented, and documentation. Where possible, automation is used to enable interoperability of tools and uniformity of baseline configurations across the information system.

2.2.3 CONTROLLING CONFIGURATION CHANGES

Given the continually evolving nature of an information system and the mission it supports, the challenge for organizations is not only to establish an initial baseline configuration that represents a secure state (which is also cost-effective, functional, and supportive of mission and business processes), but also to maintain a secure configuration in the face of the significant waves of change that ripple through organizations.

In this phase of SecCM, the emphasis is put on the management of change to maintain the secure, approved baseline of the information system. Through the use of SecCM practices, organizations ensure that changes are formally identified, proposed, reviewed, analyzed for security impact, tested, and approved prior to implementation. As part of the configuration change control effort, organizations can employ a variety of access restrictions for change including access controls, process automation, abstract layers, change windows, and verification and audit activities to limit unauthorized and/or undocumented changes to the information system.

2.2.4 MONITORING

Monitoring activities are used as the mechanism within SecCM to validate that the information system is adhering to organizational policies, procedures, and the approved secure baseline configuration. Planning and implementing secure configurations and then controlling configuration change is usually not sufficient to ensure that an information system which was once secure will remain secure. Monitoring identifies undiscovered/undocumented system components, misconfigurations, vulnerabilities, and unauthorized changes, all of which, if not addressed, can expose organizations to increased risk. Using automated tools helps organizations to efficiently identify when the information system is not consistent with the approved baseline configuration and when remediation actions are necessary. In addition, the use of automated tools often facilitates situational awareness and the documentation of deviations from the baseline configuration.

Processes and requirements within all four SecCM phases do not remain static thus all processes in all four phases are reviewed and revised as needed to support organizational risk management.

---

[13] A common secure configuration is a recognized, standardized, and established benchmark (e.g., National Checklist Program, DISA STIGs, etc.) that stipulates specific secure configuration settings for a given IT platform. See http://checklists.nist.gov.

SecCM monitoring activities may loop back to any of the previous phases (as noted in Figure 2-1) and precipitate changes.

SecCM monitoring is done through assessment and reporting activities. Reports address the secure state of individual information system configurations and are used as input to Risk Management Framework information security continuous monitoring requirements.[14] SecCM monitoring can also support gathering of information for metrics that can be used to provide quantitative evidence that the SecCM program is meeting its stated goals, and can be used to improve SecCM processes in general.

2.3   SECURITY-FOCUSED CONFIGURATION MANAGEMENT CONCEPTS

This section describes the fundamental concepts relevant to the practice of SecCM within an organization. Recognizing that organizations have widely varying missions and organizational structures, there may be differences in the way that SecCM is implemented and managed.

2.3.1   CONFIGURATION MANAGEMENT POLICY AND PROCEDURES

The development of documented SecCM policy communicates senior management's expectations for SecCM to members of the organization through specific, measurable, and confirmable objectives. It is a top-down approach which defines what is required and what is not permitted with respect to using SecCM to manage and control information resources.

While policy defines the objectives for what must be done, procedures describe how the policy objectives are met through specific actions and results. SecCM procedures are developed to describe the methodology and tasks for each activity that supports implementation of the SecCM policy.

Documenting configuration management policy and procedures is performed during the Planning phase and supports the implementation of NIST SP 800-53 control **CM-1 Configuration Management Policy and Procedures**.

2.3.2   CONFIGURATION MANAGEMENT PLAN

The Configuration Management Plan serves to describe how SecCM policy will be implemented. The SecCM Plan may be written to apply to an entire organization, or it may be localized and tailored to an information system or a group of information systems within the organization. The SecCM Plan may take the form of an all-inclusive, stand-alone document that describes all aspects of SecCM or may be contained within more broadly defined CM procedures. A SecCM Plan may also take the form of a set of documents and appendices that taken together describe all aspects of SecCM. Finally, the SecCM Plan may take the form of a set of predefined data elements in a repository.

The SecCM Plan is produced during the Planning phase and supports the implementation of NIST SP 800-53 controls **CM-1 Configuration Management Policy and Procedures** and **CM-9 Configuration Management Plan**.

---

[14] See NIST SP 800-137 for more information on information security continuous monitoring

2.3.3   CONFIGURATION CONTROL BOARD

The Configuration Control Board (CCB) is a group typically consisting of two or more individuals that have the collective responsibility and authority to review and approve changes to an information system. The group, which represents various perspectives from within the organization, is chosen to evaluate and approve changes to the information system. The CCB is a check and balance on configuration change activity, assuring that changes are held to organizationally defined criteria (e.g., scope, cost, impact on security) before being implemented.

The CCB may be less formal for information systems which have limited size, scope, and criticality in the context of the mission of the organization. The organization determines the size and formality of the CCB that is appropriate for a given information system (or systems) within the organization.

The CCB establishment is part of the Planning phase of SecCM and supports the implementation of NIST SP 800-53 control **CM-3 Configuration Change Control.**

2.3.4   COMPONENT INVENTORY

The component inventory is a descriptive record of the components within an organization down to the information system level. A consolidated representation of the components within all of the information systems within an organization allows the organization to have greater visibility into and control over its information systems, facilitating the implementation, operation, and management of a security program. The organization determines the level of granularity required for tracking the components for SecCM. For example, one organization may track a workstation (with all peripherals) as a single component while another may document each peripheral as a separate component in the inventory.

Each component is associated with only one information system and the authority over and responsibility for each component is with only one information system owner (i.e., every item in the component inventory falls within the authorization boundary of a single information system).

Creating an inventory of information system components is part of the Planning phase of SecCM and supports the implementation of the NIST SP 800-53 control **CM-8 Information System Component Inventory.**

2.3.5   CONFIGURATION ITEMS

In the context of SecCM of information systems, a *configuration item* (CI) is an aggregation of information system components that is designated for configuration management and treated as a single entity throughout the SecCM process. This implies that the CI is identified, labeled, and tracked during its life cycle – the CI is the target of many of the activities within SecCM, such as configuration change control and monitoring activities. A CI may be a specific information system component (e.g., server, workstation, router, application), a group of information system components (e.g., group of servers with like operating systems, group of network components such as routers and switches, an application or suite of applications), a non-component object (e.g., firmware, documentation), or an information system as a whole. CIs give organizations a way to decompose the information system into manageable parts whose configurations can be actively managed.

The purpose of breaking up an information system into CIs is to allow more granularity and control in managing the secure configuration of the system. The level of granularity will vary among organizations and systems and is balanced against the associated management overhead for each CI. In one organization, it may be appropriate to create a single CI to track all of the laptops within a system, while in another organization, each laptop may represent an individual CI.

Identification of the configuration items that compose an information system is part of the Planning phase of SecCM and supports the implementation of NIST SP 800-53 control **CM-3 Configuration Change Control.**

2.3.6   SECURE CONFIGURATIONS OF INFORMATION SYSTEMS

Configurations represent the possible states in which an information system and its components can be arranged. Secure configurations are designed to reduce the organizational security risk from operation of an information system, and may involve using trusted or approved software loads, maintaining up-to-date patch levels, applying secure configuration settings of the IT products used, and implementation of endpoint protection platforms. Secure configurations for an information system are most often achieved through the application of secure configuration settings to the IT products (e.g., operating systems, databases, etc.) used to build the information system. For example, a secure configuration for selected IT products used within the information system or organization could incorporate the principle of least functionality. Least functionality helps to minimize the potential for introduction of security vulnerabilities and includes, but is not limited to, disabling or uninstalling unused/unnecessary operating system (OS) functionality, protocols, ports, and services, and limiting the software that can be installed and the functionality of that software.

Implementing secure configurations is part of the Identifying and Implementing Configurations phase of SecCM and supports the implementation of NIST SP 800-53 controls **CM-6 Configuration Settings** and **CM-7 Least Functionality.**

2.3.7   BASELINE CONFIGURATION

A baseline configuration is a set of specifications for a system, or Configuration Item (CI) within a system, that has been formally reviewed and agreed on at a given point in time, and which can be changed only through change control procedures. The baseline configuration is used as a basis for future builds, releases, and/or changes.

The baseline configuration of an information system may evolve over time depending on the stage of the system development life cycle (SDLC). Early in the SDLC when an information system is being initiated and acquired, the baseline may be a set of functional requirements. As the information system is developed and implemented, the baseline may expand to include additional configuration items such as the technical design, the software load, the architecture, and configurations of the information system and its individual components. A baseline configuration may also represent different information computing environments such as development, test, and production.

When a new baseline configuration is established, the implication is that all of the changes from the last baseline have been approved. Older versions of approved baseline configurations are maintained and made available for review or rollback as needed.

Developing and documenting the baseline configuration for an information system is part of the Identifying and Implementing Configurations phase of SecCM and supports the implementation of NIST SP 800-53 control **CM-2 Baseline Configuration.**

2.3.8 CONFIGURATION CHANGE CONTROL

Configuration change control is the documented process for managing and controlling changes to the configuration of an information system or its constituent CIs. Configuration change control for the information system involves the systematic proposal, justification, implementation, test/evaluation, review, and disposition of changes to the system, including upgrades and modifications. Configuration change control is applied to include changes to components of the information system, changes to the configuration settings for information technology products, emergency/unscheduled changes, and changes to remediate flaws. Changes are controlled from the time the change is proposed to the implementation and testing of the change. Each step in the change process is clearly articulated along with the responsibilities and authorities of the roles involved.

Configuration change control falls under the Controlling Configuration Changes phase of SecCM and supports the implementation of NIST SP 800-53 control **CM-3 Configuration Change Control** and **CM-5 Access Restrictions for Change**.

2.3.9 SECURITY IMPACT ANALYSIS

Security impact analysis is the analysis conducted by qualified staff within an organization to determine the extent to which changes to the information system affect the security posture of the system. Because information systems are typically in a constant state of change, it is important to understand the impact of changes on the functionality of existing security controls and in the context of organizational risk tolerance. Security impact analysis is incorporated into the documented configuration change control process.

The analysis of the security impact of a change occurs when changes are analyzed and evaluated for adverse impact on security, preferably before they are approved and implemented, but also in the case of emergency/unscheduled changes. Once the changes are implemented and tested, a security impact analysis (and/or assessment) is performed to ensure that the changes have been implemented as approved, and to determine if there are any unanticipated effects of the change on existing security controls.

Security impact analysis is performed as a part of the Controlling Configuration Changes phase of SecCM and supports the implementation of NIST SP 800-53 control **CM-4 Security Impact Analysis.**

2.3.10 CONFIGURATION MONITORING

Configuration monitoring involves activities to determine whether information systems are configured in accordance with the organization's agreed-upon baseline configurations, and whether the IS components identified within the information system are consistent with the IS component inventory being maintained by the organization.

Configuration monitoring helps to ensure that SecCM controls are operating as intended and are providing effective security while supporting adherence to SecCM policies and procedures. Configuration monitoring may also help to motivate staff members to perform SecCM activities in accordance with policies and procedures. Additionally, configuration monitoring supports organizations in their efforts to conform to the Risk Management Framework.[15] Information

---

[15] See NIST SP 800-37, as amended, for more information on the Risk Management Framework (RMF).

gathered during configuration monitoring can be used to support overall continuous monitoring activities[16] including ongoing assessments of specific security controls and updates to security documentation such as System Security Plans, Security Assessment Reports, and Security Status Reports. Automation capabilities, such as those defined by SCAP, can be used to automate assessment activities.

Configuration monitoring is part of the Monitoring phase of SecCM and supports the implementation of **all NIST SP 800-53 controls in the CM Family**.

2.4   SECCM ROLES AND RESPONSIBILITIES

The set of roles (at the organizational as well as the information system level) that are relevant to the SecCM program are defined along with the responsibilities. The responsibilities are in the context of SecCM only and are not inclusive of other non-SecCM responsibilities the roles may also have. Typically, SecCM roles and responsibilities include:

Chief Information Officer (CIO)
The CIO designates and/or provides a SecCM Program Manager for the organization and approves the organizational SecCM plan and policies.

Senior Information Security Officer (SISO)
The SISO may act as the SecCM Program Manager for the organization. The SISO may also provide staff with security expertise to serve on the CCB and/or to conduct security impact analyses. Organizations may also refer to this position as the Chief Information Security Officer (CISO).

Authorizing Official (AO)
The AO manages or participates in the CCB for systems s/he authorizes and may provide technical staff to conduct and/or review security impact analyses. The AO coordinates with the Risk Executive (Function) on SecCM issues and makes the final determination whether or not a given change or set of changes continues to be an acceptable security risk.

Information System Owner (ISO)
The ISO identifies, defines, and ensures implementation of the aspects of SecCM for the information system that have not been defined by the organization of which the information system is a part. The ISO also ensures implementation of organizational-level SecCM requirements for the information system.

SecCM Program Manager
The SecCM Program Manager develops SecCM policies and procedures, provides direction, and oversees the implementation of the SecCM program for the organization and/or system level SecCM program. The SecCM Program Manager may be the SISO (or someone designated by the SISO or the CIO) at the organizational level or the ISO (or someone designated by the ISO) at the system level.

Information System Security Officer (ISSO)
The ISSO assists the information system owner with implementation of SecCM for the system, conducts configuration monitoring activities (reporting and analysis), and may serve on the CCB.

---

[16] See Draft NIST SP 800-137 for more information on continuous monitoring (Step Six in the RMF).

Information System Administrator (ISA)

The ISA implements agreed-upon secure baseline configurations, incorporates secure configuration settings for IT products, and assists with security impact analyses and configuration monitoring activities as needed. In addition, the ISA may be included in the process for determining the appropriate baseline configuration for each CI and may serve on the CCB. ISAs are also responsible for complying with SecCM policies and implementing/following SecCM procedures.

System/Software Developer

The developer ensures that secure configuration settings are built into applications in accordance with security requirements and assists with security impact analyses and configuration monitoring activities as needed. In addition, the developer may be included in the process for determining the appropriate baseline configuration for relevant CIs and may serve on the CCB. Developers are also responsible for complying with SecCM policies and implementing/following SecCM procedures.

Information System User (ISU)

The ISU initiates change requests, assists with functional testing, and complies with SecCM requirements.

CHAPTER THREE

THE PROCESS
IMPLEMENTATION AND APPLICATION OF SECURITY-FOCUSED CONFIGURATION MANAGEMENT

This chapter describes the process of applying security-focused configuration management to information systems within an organization. The goal of SecCM activities is to manage and monitor the configurations of information systems to achieve adequate security and minimize organizational risk while supporting the desired business functionality and services.

The following sections discuss activities that occur within each of the four phases of SecCM. Some of these activities may be more efficiently performed at the organizational level (i.e., applying to more than one information system), while other activities may be more efficiently performed at the system level (i.e., applying to a single information system). Each organization determines what activities are conducted at the organizational level and what activities are conducted at the system level in accordance with organizational management requirements. Appendix G provides flow charts of the SecCM activities described here. The flow charts are intended to serve as tools for organizations to draw upon for developing their own organizational and information system SecCM processes.

3.1 PLANNING

This section describes various SecCM planning activities at both the organizational and information system level.

3.1.1 PLANNING AT THE ORGANIZATIONAL LEVEL

The following subsections describe the *planning* phase activities that are normally conducted at the organizational level. The subsections are listed in the order in which the planning activities typically occur. As always, organizations have flexibility in determining which activities are performed at what level and in what order. Planning at the organizational level includes SecCM program documented policies and procedures that provide direction and support for managing configurations of individual information systems within the organization.

Establish Organization-wide SecCM Program

The practice of SecCM for ensuring adequate security and facilitating the management of risk is most effectively realized if it is implemented in a consistent manner across the organization. Some SecCM activities are more effective when performed at the organizational level, with responsibility assigned to the organization-wide SecCM program.

For organizations with varied and complex enterprise architecture, implementing SecCM in a consistent and uniform manner across the organization requires organization-wide coordination of resources. A senior management-level program manager designated to lead and oversee the organization-wide SecCM program can provide this type of coordination. For many large organizations, dedicated staff may be needed. For smaller organizations, or those with funding or resource constraints, the organization-wide SecCM program may be implemented by senior management-level staff that meet as a group to determine the SecCM-related activities for the organization.

The SecCM program manager provides knowledge and direction in the form of policies and procedures, communications, training, defined roles and responsibilities, support, oversight of program activities, and coordination with stakeholders. An organization-wide SecCM program also demonstrates management commitment for the effort. This commitment from the top of the organization is communicated throughout the organization down to the individual information system owners.

The SecCM program manager facilitates communications regarding SecCM policies, procedures, issues, etc., within the organization. Consideration is given to implementation of a security information management console or "dashboard" to communicate basic project and operational information to stakeholders in language they understand. The SecCM program manager also considers other vehicles for communication such as Web site updates, emails, and newsletters to share milestones, measures of value, and other SecCM-related news with stakeholders.

Primary Roles: SecCM Program Manager

Supporting Roles: SISO (if s/he is not the SecCM Program Manager); CIO; AO

Expected Input: Organizational risk tolerance; organizational security requirements; applicable laws, regulations, policies, etc. from higher authorities

Expected Output: Functional organization-wide SecCM program

Develop Organizational SecCM Policy

The organization is typically responsible for defining documented policies for the SecCM program. The SecCM program manager develops, disseminates, and periodically reviews and updates the SecCM policies for the organization. The policies are included as a part of the overall organization-wide security policy. The SecCM policy normally includes the following:

- Purpose – the objective(s) in establishing organization-wide SecCM policy;
- Scope – the extent of the enterprise architecture to which the policy applies;
- Roles – the roles that are significant within the context of the policy;
- Responsibilities – the responsibilities of each identified role;
- Activities – the functions that are performed to meet policy objectives;
- Common secure configurations – federal and/or organization-wide standardized benchmarks for configuration settings along with how to address deviations; and
- Records – the records of configuration management activities to be maintained; the information to be included in each type of record; who is responsible for writing/keeping the records; and procedures for protecting, accessing, auditing, and ultimately deleting such records.

SecCM policy may also address the following topics:

- SecCM training requirements;
- Use of SecCM templates;
- Use of automated tools;
- Prohibited configuration settings; and
- Requirements for inventory of information systems and components.

The SecCM policy emphasizes management commitment, clarifies the required level of coordination among organizational entities, and defines the configuration monitoring approach.

Primary Roles: SecCM Program Manager

Supporting Roles: SISO (if s/he is not the SecCM Program Manager); CIO; AO

Expected Input: Organizational risk tolerance; organizational security requirements; applicable laws, regulations, policies, etc. from higher authorities

Expected Output: Documented SecCM policies

Develop Organizational SecCM Procedures

The organization typically establishes and maintains common procedures for security-focused configuration management activities; however, some SecCM procedures may require development at the system level. Organizations may also provide hybrid procedures, i.e., the organization establishes procedures that contain parameters to be defined at the system level. In any case, the procedures are documented and disseminated to relevant staff, and in accordance with organizational policy. SecCM procedures address the following, as applicable:

Templates - Establishes templates related to SecCM that integrate the organization-wide SecCM policy and procedures and allow individual system owners to fill in information specific to their information system. Templates may be developed for a SecCM Plan, system-specific procedure(s), change requests, security impact analyses, reporting on SecCM, etc. Templates may also be developed to apply specifically to low, moderate, or high-impact information systems.[17] Sample templates are provided in Appendices D and E.

IS Component Inventory – Describes how components are to be managed within the inventory (e.g., how new components are added to the inventory, what information about each component is tracked, and how updates are made including removal of retired components). If automated tools are to be used, factors such as how often they will run, who will administer them, who will have access, and how they will be audited are described.

Baseline Configuration – Identifies the steps for creation of a baseline configuration, content of the baseline configuration, approval of the initial baseline configuration, maintenance of the baseline configuration (i.e., when it should be updated and by whom), and control of the baseline configuration. If applicable, requirements from higher regulatory bodies are considered and integrated when defining baseline configurations (e.g., requirements from OMB memos, laws such as Health Insurance Portability and Accountability Act (HIPAA), etc.).

Common Secure Configurations – Identifies commonly recognized and standardized secure configurations to be applied to configuration items. The common secure configurations specified in the procedure are derived from established federal, organizational, or industry specifications (the National Checklist Program contains references to common secure configurations such as the United States Government Configuration Baseline (USGCB), Federal Desktop Core Configuration (FDCC), Defense Information System Agency (DISA) Security Technical

---

[17] Information systems categorized in accordance with FIPS 199, *Standards for Categorization of Federal Information and Information Systems*, and the security impact level derived from the categorization in accordance with FIPS 200, *Minimum Security Requirements for Federal Information and Information Systems.*

Implementation Guides (STIGs), Center for Internet Security (CIS) Benchmarks, etc.). Where possible, common secure configurations use SCAP-expressed content. Deviations from the common secure configurations are also addressed (e.g., identification of acceptable methods for assessing, approving, documenting, and justifying deviations to common secure configurations, along with identification of controls implemented to mitigate risk from the deviations), in the event that the configuration for a given system must diverge from the defined configuration due to mission requirements or other constraints.

Patch Management – Defines how an organization's patch management process is integrated into SecCM, how patches are prioritized and approved through the configuration change control process, and how patches are tested for their impact on existing secure configurations. Also defines how patches are integrated into updates to approved baseline configurations and how patch implementation is controlled (access controls, etc.).

Configuration Change Control – Identifies the steps to move a configuration change from its initial request to eventual release into the operational environment. The procedure includes, but is not limited to:

- Change request and approval procedures;
- Criteria to determine the types of changes that are preapproved or exempt from configuration control such as vendor-provided security patches, updated antivirus signatures, creation or deletion of users, replacement of defective peripherals, motherboard or hard drives, etc.;[18]
- Security impact analysis procedures including how and with what level of rigor analysis results are to be documented and requirements for post-implementation review to confirm that the change was implemented as approved and that no additional security impact has resulted;
- Criteria to determine whether a change is significant enough to trigger consideration of system reauthorization activities;
- Review for consistency with organizational enterprise architecture;
- Establishment of a group that approves changes (e.g., a Configuration Control Board);
- Requirements for testing of changes for submission to the CCB (i.e., the format and types of information to present to the CCB such as a test plan, schedule, and test results);
- If change approvals at the system level are permitted, criteria for elevating a change request from system level approval to organizational approval (e.g., the change will affect other organizational systems, the change will require a system outage that could adversely impact the mission, etc.);
- Requirements for testing of changes prior to release into the operational environment;
- Requirements for access restrictions for change (i.e., who can make change to the information system and under what circumstances);
- Requirements for rollback of changes in the event that problems occur;
- Requirements for management of unscheduled changes (e.g., changes needed for critical flaw remediation) that are tailored to support expedited reviews and approvals; and
- Requirements for retroactive analysis, testing, and approval of changes that are implemented outside of the change control process.

---

[18] Preapproved changes are still tested and documented prior to implementation.

Help Desk Procedures – Describes how change requests originating through the help desk are recorded, submitted, tracked, and integrated into the configuration change control process.

SDLC Procedures – Describes how SecCM is used to manage and control system configurations and changes within the organizationally defined SDLC process and throughout the life cycle of a system.

Monitoring – Describes how monitoring activities and related reports are applied to assess the secure state of the information system, and how to identify when the actual configuration becomes different in some way from the approved baseline configuration (i.e., unauthorized change) within an information system through analysis of monitoring and reporting activities.

Media Library Procedures – Describes management of the media library and includes naming conventions for media, labeling procedures (name/version, date created, retention period, owner, date for destruction, impact or classification level), tracking media, access controls, protections for media integrity (e.g., checksums), inventory checks, capacity planning, and archiving of media.

Primary Roles: SecCM Program Manager; ISOs. Note: SecCM Program Managers and ISOs both have responsibility in determining which procedures are needed at their respective levels and how they are documented (e.g., as several separate procedures, as a single procedure, as part of the SecCM plan)

Supporting Roles: SISO or equivalent (if s/he is not the SecCM Program Manager); ISSO; ISA; User

Expected Input: Organizational policies organizational risk tolerance; organizational security requirements; applicable laws, regulations, policies, etc. from higher authorities

Expected Output: Documented SecCM procedures

Develop the SecCM Monitoring Strategy

SecCM monitoring verifies that the SecCM process is effective with respect to maintaining the security posture of the organization and adherence to baseline configurations and SecCM policy. The SecCM monitoring strategy is based on the risk tolerance of, and security requirements for, the organization. The SecCM monitoring strategy is consistent with, and provides input to, the organization's overall continuous monitoring strategy. The organization typically develops the SecCM monitoring strategy; however, organizations have the flexibility to develop some or all of the SecCM monitoring strategy at the system level.

A schedule for SecCM monitoring and associated reporting is established as part of the strategy. Scheduled and ad hoc assessments are included within the strategy. The monitoring schedule may coincide with scheduled releases such that assessments are performed before and after deployments. Ad hoc assessments may also be conducted so that staff does not become lax in between scheduled assessments. Additionally, the schedule includes provisions for reviewing and revising the SecCM monitoring strategy to ensure that the strategy continues to meet organizational security requirements.

See Section 3.4 for more information on SecCM monitoring.

Primary Roles: SecCM Program Manager

Supporting Roles: SISO or equivalent (if s/he is not the SecCM Program Manager); ISO; ISSO

Expected Input: SecCM policy and procedures, overall organizational continuous monitoring policy and procedures; organizational risk tolerance; organizational security requirements

Expected Output: Strategy and schedule for configuration monitoring and reporting

Define the Types of Changes That Do Not Require Configuration Change Control

In the interest of resource management, the organization may wish to designate the types of changes that are preapproved (i.e., changes that are not sent to the CCB for approval)[18] and changes that are typically *not* included under configuration control (i.e., changes that are completely exempt from SecCM). Vendor-provided security patches, updated antivirus signatures, and replacement of defective peripherals or internal hardware are examples of changes that may be preapproved. Database content updates, creating/removing/updating accounts, and creation or deletion of user files are examples of changes that are typically exempt from configuration change control.

Primary Roles: SecCM Program Manager; ISO

Supporting Roles: SISO (if s/he is not the SecCM Program Manager); AO; ISSO; ISA; System/Software Developers

Expected Input: SecCM policies and procedures; types of changes that typically occur within the organization and/or system

Expected Output: Record of the types of changes that are exempt from configuration control; record of the types of changes that are configuration controlled

Develop SecCM Training

SecCM is a fundamental part of an organizational security program, but often requires a change in organizational culture. Staff is provided training to ensure their understanding of SecCM policies and procedures. Training also provides a venue for management to communicate the reasons why SecCM is important. SecCM training material is developed covering organizational policies, procedures, tools, artifacts, and monitoring requirements. The training may be mandatory or optional as appropriate and is targeted to relevant staff (e.g., system administrators, system/software developers, system security officers, system owners, etc.) as necessary to ensure that staff has the skills to manage the baseline configurations in accordance with organizational policy.

Primary Roles: SecCM Program Manager; ISO

Supporting Roles: SISO (if s/he is not the SecCM Program Manager); CIO; AO; ISSO

Expected Input: SecCM policies and procedures

Expected Output: Training materials and/or courses scheduled as necessary

Identify Approved IT Products

Many organizations establish a list of approved hardware and software products for use across the organization. Information system owners are able to select and use products from the approved list without the need for explicit approval. Depending upon organizational policy, additional products required for a particular information system may need to be approved by the CCB for that information system; alternatively, a product used may need to be added to the organizationally controlled and approved IT products list. Some organizations may also provide a buying service or similar purchasing/contracting vehicle from which preapproved products may be purchased or are required to be purchased.

Primary Roles: SecCM Program Manager and/or the Configuration Control Board; ISO

Supporting Roles: SISO (if s/he is not the SecCM Program Manager); AO; ISSO

Expected Input: SecCM policies and procedures; organizational security requirements; acquisition/buying service information

Expected Output: List of approved IT Products for the organization

Identify Tools

Managing the myriad configurations found within information system components has become an almost impossible task using manual methods like spreadsheets. When possible, organizations look for automated solutions which, in the long run, can lower costs, enhance efficiency, and improve the reliability of SecCM efforts.

In most cases, tools to support activities in SecCM phases two, three, and four are selected for use across the organization by SecCM program management, and information system owners are responsible for applying the tools to the SecCM activities performed on each information system. Similarly, tools and mechanisms for inventory reporting and management may be provided to information system owners by the organization. In accordance with federal government and organizational policy, if automated tools are used, the tools are Security Content Automation Protocol (SCAP)-validated to the extent that such tools are available. SCAP is described in more detail in Section 3.5.

If not provided by the organization, tools are identified and deployed to support SecCM at the information system level. When possible, existing SecCM tools from within the organization are leveraged to support consistent organization-wide SecCM practices, centralized reporting, and cost efficiency. Leveraging existing tools may require them to be installed and configured to function on individual information systems. This usually requires that accounts be set up, administrators identified, schedules determined, the appropriate baseline configurations set up, and possibly installation of a client on each component to be configuration-controlled. If the tool has already been deployed within the organization, instructions for installation, configuration, and deployment are available or easy to produce if needed.

There are a wide variety of configuration management tools available to support an organization's SecCM program. At a minimum, the organization considers tools that can automatically assess configuration settings of IS components. Automated tools should be able to scan different information system components (e.g., Web server, database server, network devices, etc.) running different operating systems, identify the current configuration settings, and indicate where they are noncompliant with policy. Such tools import settings from one or more common secure configurations and then allow for tailoring the configurations to the organization's security and mission/functional requirements.

Tools that implement and/or assess configuration settings are evaluated to determine whether they include requirements such as:

- Ability to pull information from a variety of sources (different type of components, different operating systems, different platforms, etc.);
- Use of standardized specifications such as XML and SCAP;
- Integration with other products such as help desk, inventory management, and incident response solutions;
- Vendor-provided support (patches, updated vulnerability signatures, etc.);
- Compliance with applicable federal laws, Executive Orders, directives, policies, regulations, standards, and guidelines and link vulnerabilities to SP 800-53 controls;
- Standardized reporting capability (e.g. SCAP, XML) including the ability to tailor output and drill down; and
- Data consolidation into Security Information and Event Management (SIEM) tools and dashboard products.

Organizations may consider implementation of an all-in-one solution for configuration management. For example, various configuration management functions are included in products for managing IT servers, workstations, desktops, and services provided by applications. These products may include functions such as:

- Inventory/discovery of IS components;
- Software distribution;
- Patch management;
- Operating system deployment;
- Policy management;
- Migration to new baseline configuration; and
- Backup/recovery.

Primary Roles: SecCM Program Manager and/or the Configuration Control Board; ISO

Supporting Roles: SISO (if s/he is not the SecCM Program Manager); CIO; AO; ISSO; ISA

Expected Input: SecCM policies and procedures; organizational and information system security requirements; acquisition/buying service information

Expected Output: Tools to be implemented in support of SecCM

Establish Configuration Test Environment and Program

Some organizations may wish to establish and maintain a configuration test environment and program for testing IT products, tools, and proposed changes to them in a centrally managed environment isolated from the production environment. The test environment is used for various types of testing to include:

- IT products proposed for approval and use within the organization;
- Configuration settings for approved IT products;

- Patches issued by suppliers prior to their rollout through the organization;
- Validation of tools that detect unapproved configuration settings;
- Verification of testing processes to validate approved configuration settings;
- Security impact analyses; and
- Other configuration-related changes.

NIST SP 800-115, *Technical Guide to Information Security Testing and Assessment*, provides guidelines on how to establish and conduct an effective information security functional testing program. Specific guidelines are provided for system configuration review and vulnerability scanning which may be directly applied to the configuration test program.

Primary Roles: SecCM Program Manager; ISO

Supporting Roles: SISO (if s/he is not the SecCM Program Manager); CIO; AO; ISSO; ISA

Expected Input: SecCM policies and procedures;

Expected Output: Isolated test environment and program in support of SecCM

3.1.2 PLANNING AT THE SYSTEM LEVEL

The following subsections describe the *planning* phase activities that are normally completed at the system level. The subsections are listed in the order in which the planning activities typically occur. As always, organizations have flexibility in determining which activities are performed at the organizational level and which activities are performed at the system level, and in what order. The system-level planning phase results in a completed SecCM Plan, an established Configuration Control Board, an accurate information system component inventory, and defined configuration items for the system.

Develop SecCM Plan for Information System

The primary goal of the SecCM Plan is to document or provide references to system-specific SecCM-related information. The organization may define a master SecCM Plan and provide templates that require a subset of the SecCM Plan to be documented for each information system, or the system owner may be required to define the system SecCM Plan in its entirety. Regardless of the format, a SecCM Plan is completed at the system level and typically covers the following topics:

- Brief description of the subject information system;
- Information system component inventory;
- Information system configuration items;
- Rigor to be applied to managing changes to configuration items (e.g., based on the impact level of the information system[19]);
- Identification of the roles and responsibilities;
- Identification and composition of the group or individual(s) that consider change

---

[19] Information systems categorized in accordance with FIPS 199, *Standards for Categorization of Federal Information and Information Systems*, and FIPS 200, *Minimum Security Requirements for Federal Information and Information Systems.*

requests;
- Configuration change control procedures to be followed (including references to organization-wide procedures);
- Identification on the location where SecCM artifacts (change requests, approvals, etc.) are maintained (e.g., media libraries);
- Access controls employed to control changes to configurations;
- Access controls to protect SecCM artifacts, records, reports, etc. (e.g., commensurate with system impact level;
- SecCM tools that are used;
- Identification of common secure configurations (e.g., FDCC/USGCB, DISA STIGs, National Checklist Program, etc.) to be used as a basis for establishing approved baseline configurations for the information system;
- Deviations from common secure configurations for configuration items including justifications;
- Criteria for approving baseline configurations for the information system; and
- Handling of exceptions to the SecCM plan (e.g., location of SecCM artifacts, configuration change control procedures, etc.).

The SecCM Plan may have various representations; it could be an actual document, a collection of data stored within a SecCM tool, or a variety of other representations. SecCM procedures may be covered separately or the SecCM plan may incorporate SecCM procedures. The SecCM Plan may also be instantiated at the system level from organizational templates. The level of detail for the SecCM plan is commensurate with the impact level of the subject information system.

SDLC Phase: Begin in Initiation phase, fine tune in Development/Acquisition phase, finalize in Implementation/Assessment phase

Primary Roles: ISO

Supporting Roles: ISSO; ISA; System/Software Developer; User

Expected Input: Organizational SecCM policies, procedures, and templates

Expected Output: System-level SecCM plan, including system-level procedures

Create or Update Information System Component Inventory

An information system component is a discrete identifiable IT asset that represents a building block of an information system. An accurate component inventory is essential to record the components that compose the information system. The component inventory helps to improve the security of the information system by providing a comprehensive view of the components that need to be managed and secured. All information system components are tracked from acquisition to retirement as part of the organization's SDLC process.

The information system component inventory can be represented as:

$$\text{IS Component Inventory} = \{ISC_1, ISC_2, \dots ISC_n\},$$

where n is greater than or equal to one, and ISC represents an information system component within the organization.

Every organizational component is included within the authorization boundary of one, and only one, information system and is documented and tracked in an inventory which reflects the association with the information system under which it is managed i.e., an component associated with an information system is included in that information system component inventory. A component may support information systems that are not within the same authorization boundary (such as a server that supports several Web applications or virtual machines); however, the owners of the supported information systems have neither authority over, nor responsibility for, the supporting component and thus the component would not be included in the component inventories of the supported information systems.

The component inventory is populated through a process of discovery. Discovery, which may be manual or automated, is the process of obtaining information on IS components that compose the information systems within the organization. The organization typically determines the types and granularity of the components (peripherals versus workstations, routers, etc.) that are to be identified within the inventory. In most organizations, it is impractical to manually collect this information for inclusion in the inventory or for analysis against the authorized inventory. The use of automated tools for discovery, analysis, and management of component inventories is generally a more effective and efficient means of maintaining component inventories. Still, it is important to note that even with automated inventory management tools, it may still be necessary to enter some component inventory data elements manually. Examples include, but are not limited to, organizational unique identifiers, information system association (depending on network configuration, whether the inventory management tool installation is at the organizational level or system level, etc.), system/component owner, administrator, or user, configuration item association, or type of component. Tools that support inventory management are usually database-driven applications to track and manage information system components within a given environment. Once an inventory is established, automated tools are often used to detect the removal or addition of components. Some inventory management tools allow for expanded monitoring of components through the use of built-in hooks in the OS, installation of agents on each component, or Application Programming Interfaces. With this functionality, the inventory management system can monitor changes in the component's configuration and report the results to specified staff.

Inventory management tools are SCAP-validated, to the extent such tools are available. When purchasing a commercial off-the-shelf (COTS) or customized inventory management application, organizations are well advised to include SCAP requirements in requests for proposals, purchase agreements, contracts, etc. Specifying components by a commonly recognized identifier such as the Common Platform Enumeration (CPE) can facilitate interchange of data among SCAP-compliant tools. See Section 3.5 for more information on SCAP. Use of commonly recognized identifiers from the start of the acquisition process provides a common taxonomy for the component inventory to track components throughout the entire SDLC (i.e., from acquisition to retirement).

An IS component inventory adds real value to SecCM when each item in the inventory is associated with information that can be leveraged for determination of approved configuration baselines, configuration change control/security impact analysis, and monitoring/reporting. Some data elements[20] typically stored for each component in the IS component inventory include:

- Unique Identifier and/or Serial Number;

---

[20] See NISTIR 7693, *Specifications for Asset Identification 1.1* for information on specifications for data elements.

- Information System of which the component is a part;[21]
- Type of IS component (e.g., server, desktop, application);
- Manufacturer/Model information;
- Operating System Type and Version/Service Pack Level (preferably using the appropriate Common Platform Enumeration Name);
- Presence of virtual machines;[21]
- Application Software Version/License information (preferably using the appropriate Common Platform Enumeration Name);
- Physical location (e.g., building/room number);
- Logical location (e.g., IP address);
- Media Access Control (MAC) address;
- Owner;
- Operational status;
- Primary and secondary administrators; and
- Primary user (if applicable).

Some additional data elements may also be recorded to facilitate SecCM, such as:

- Status of the component (e.g., operational, spare, disposed, etc.);
- Relationships to other IS components in the inventory;[21]
- Relationships to/dependencies on other information systems;[21]
- Other information systems supported by this component;[21]
- Identification of any Service-Level Agreements (SLA) that apply to the component;
- Applicable common secure configurations;
- Configuration item (CI) of which it is a part;
- Security controls supported by this component; and
- Identification of any incident logs that apply to the component.

SDLC Phase: Begin in Development/Acquisition phase, finalize in Implementation/Assessment phase, ongoing updates during Operations and Maintenance phase

Primary Roles: ISO

Supporting Roles: ISSO; ISA; ISU

Expected Input: Organizational and/or system-level tools, organizational and/or system-level policies and procedures

Expected Output: Accurate IS component inventory

---

[21] A single IS component may support additional information systems. For example, a server in a server farm may host several virtual machines, and each virtual machine in turn may support a Web application. When such a server suffers a service interruption or compromise, the information stored in the component inventory about the uses of that server can assist in the quick identification of the applications that are impacted so that appropriate actions can be taken. Additionally, virtual machines are included as separate items in IS component inventories and are under configuration control. Identifying virtual machines and including them in the CM process is important in managing overall organizational risk and system-level security.

Determine Configuration Items

When implementing configuration management, the system owner determines how to best decompose the information system (IS) into one or more configuration items (CIs). CIs may be one or a group of IS components, documents, network diagrams, scripts, custom code, and various other elements that compose the information system and which require configuration management.

An IS can be represented as a set of one or more CIs as follows:

$$IS = \{CI_1, CI_2, ...CI_n\} \text{ where } n \text{ is greater than or equal to } 1.$$

There is a one-to-many relationship between ISs and CIs. Thus, each IS is composed of one or more CIs and each CI is part of one, and only one, IS. In cases where an organization establishes and maintains a common configuration baseline for a given platform (e.g., Windows version X, Linux version Y) or component type (e.g., workstation, server, router) each individual information system inherits the common configuration baseline as a CI, or part of a CI, for that information system. The CI is managed for use in that information system to include any deviations as justified and recorded (See Section 3.2.2.iii). The point is that a CI is owned and managed as part of only one IS regardless of the common configuration baseline source.

A CI may be composed of one or more IS components (ISCs) (e.g., server, workstation, router, application), one or more non-component (NC) information system objects (e.g., documentation, diagrams, firmware), or some combination thereof as indicated in the following representations:

    i. $CI_A = \{ISC_1, ISC_2, ...ISC_n\}$ where n is greater than or equal to one;

    ii. $CI_B = \{NC_1, NC_2, ...NC_n\}$ where n is greater than or equal to one; and/or

    iii. $CI_C = \{ISC_1, ISC_2, ...ISC_n + NC_1, NC_2, ...NC_n\}$ where n is greater than or equal to one.

For example, an information system with a number of servers using similar technology may be taken together as one CI (as in representation i). System applications may be represented as one or more CIs (also as in representation i). All documentation for the system may be included in one CI or each document may be treated as a separate CI (as in representation ii). Conversely, the system owner may find that it is more expedient to include the servers, applications running on the servers, and supporting documentation in a single CI (as in representation iii). When applying representations i or ii, it is important to note that the rigor of the review and approval of change proposals for one CI (e.g., a CI composed of servers) may be higher than that applied to another CI (e.g., a CI composed of documentation). Furthermore, CIs within the same system may be tracked using different tools.

Every item within the IS component inventory is associated with one and only one CI, and hence, is included within the authorization boundary of a single information system.

Each CI is assigned an unambiguous identifier so that it can be uniquely referenced within SecCM processes. Each CI could have a series of approved baseline configurations as it moves through its life cycle and is the object of configuration change control. As the CI moves through its life cycle, the organization manages version numbers for the CI.

A set of data elements is maintained for each CI to define and describe the CI to enable it to be rebuilt from scratch. The types of information that are associated with a CI may include:

- The information system of which the CI is a part;
- Logical and/or physical placement within the system;
- Ownership and management information;
- Inventory of IS components that makes up the CI;
- Inventory of documentation that makes up the CI;
- Version numbers for components and non-component objects;
- Relationship to/dependencies on other CIs within the system;
- Information related to custom software used within the CI;
- IT products or components common secure configurations; and
- Any other information needed to rebuild or reconstitute the CI.

While decomposing an information system into a number of CIs may make it easier to manage changes within the information system, it is important to note that when one CI within an IS changes, other CIs within the IS may also be affected. Furthermore, approved changes to a CI may result in updates to the system IS component inventory.

Another potential type of configuration item that is considered, particularly with respect to establishment and maintenance of a configuration test program is a CI for SecCM tools and testing processes. Tools and testing processes used to validate deviations from approved information system baseline configurations are under configuration control to reduce the potential for such testing to return false positive or false negative results (i.e., subject tools and processes are able to detect unauthorized configuration settings and are able to successfully recognize approved configuration settings).

SDLC Phase: Begin in Development/Acquisition phase, finalize in Implementation/Assessment phase

Primary Roles: ISO

Supporting Roles: ISSO; ISA

Expected Input: Organizational and/or system level policies and procedures; IS component inventory; IS documents; IS diagrams; IS scripts; IS custom code; any other IS elements that require configuration management

Expected Output: IS components and non-component objects grouped into CIs

Relationship between an Information System and Its Configuration Items and Information System Components

Figure 3-1 depicts the relationship between the information system as a whole, individual information system components and non-component objects, and information system configuration items (CIs). The information system is composed of numerous individual components and non-component objects as described above. The information system components and non-component objects that require configuration management are grouped into CIs whose configurations are managed as one. For instance, in Figure 3-1 at the component level we see numerous individual desktops. At the CI level we see that all the desktops running OS QRS version 8 have been grouped into one CI and all the desktops running OS XYZ version 5 have been grouped into another CI. In this way, the system components and non-component objects with related/similar/identical configuration requirements are configuration-managed as a group rather than as individual components.

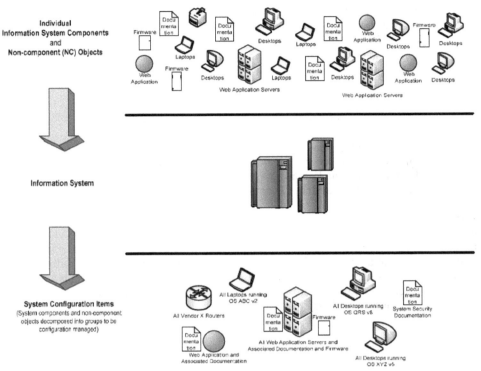

Figure 3-1 – Example of the Relationship between an IS and its Components and CIs

Establish Configuration Control Board (CCB) for Information System

A CCB or equivalent group is identified for the review and approval of configuration changes for the information system. The CCB is established through the creation of a charter which defines the authority and scope of the group and how it should operate. A charter may define the CCB's membership, the roles and responsibilities of its members, and whether it reports to an oversight body like an Executive Steering Committee or the Risk Executive (Function). A charter also describes the process by which the CCB operates, including how to handle changes and the range of dispositions (approved, not approved, on hold, etc.), evaluation criteria, and the quorum required to make configuration change control-related decisions.

The CCB plays an important role of gatekeeper in deciding which changes may be acted upon and introduced into an information system. The CCB deliberately considers the potential effect of a proposed change on the functionality and secure state of the information system and risk to the mission should the change be implemented in the context of the risk tolerance established by the organization. By reviewing each proposed and implemented modification, the CCB ensures that there is a disciplined, systematic, and secure approach for introducing change. Having a clearly defined process or framework for the evaluation and approval of change requests, including predefined evaluation criteria, helps to ensure that each proposed and implemented change is evaluated in a consistent and repeatable manner balancing security, business, and technical viewpoints.

Organizational policy may allow flexibility regarding the size and formality of the CCB. Low-impact and/or small, uncomplicated information systems may require less formality such that the CCB may be composed of as few as two members (typically the system owner and the ISSO). For high-impact systems and complex moderate-impact systems, the organization may require a CCB that is composed of at least three individuals, at least one of whom is an ISSO or ISSM. Additionally, the organization may determine that it is necessary to formally submit proposed changes to the CCB and go through formalized reviews and security impact analysis prior to acceptance and approval.

Regardless of the size and formalism of the CCB for an information system, best practices for configuration change control require that changes to the information system be vetted by at least one authorized individual who is independent of the requestor – in other words, in order to maintain adequate separation of duties, system administrators, developers, etc., are not given the authority to unilaterally propose and approve changes to the configuration of an information system (excluding changes identified in procedures as being exempt from SecCM). The vetting activity is recorded in an artifact that can be archived (e.g., CCB minutes, actions to be taken, assigned responsibilities for actions, reports generated, approvals/disapprovals and rationale, etc.).

In selecting members of the CCB, an organization considers roles that represent a range of stakeholders. The viewpoints and expertise of individuals representing the organizational and/or system mission, information security (information system security officers, security architects, etc.), information technology (e.g., system administrators, network engineers, enterprise architects, etc.), end users, customers, vendors, etc., are considered for inclusion in the CCB. It is not necessary that all participants have a voting role in the CCB, but their input may support improved decision making. For example, vendor participation may be valuable for insight into product-specific functions, features, or configurations but the vendor is not given a vote on approval of the change.

SDLC Phase: Begin in Development/Acquisition phase, finalize in Implementation/Assessment phase

Primary Roles: SecCM Program Manager (if established at the organizational level); ISO (if established at the system level). Note: If a single CCB serves a number of information systems but is not at the organizational level, the set of ISOs for all of the participating information systems are responsible for implementing the CCB

Supporting Roles: SISO (if s/he is not the SecCM Program Manager); ISSO

Expected Input: Organizational and/or system-level policies and procedures

Expected Output: Established Configuration Control Board and charter

3.2 IDENTIFYING AND IMPLEMENTING CONFIGURATIONS

The following subsections describe the *Identifying and Implementing Configurations* phase activities. In this phase, the activities are typically completed at the system level following the applicable organizational and/or system-specific SecCM policy and procedures. The subsections are listed in the general chronological order in which the configuration activities occur. As always, organizations have flexibility in determining which activities are performed at what level and in what order. Completion of the Identifying and Implementing Configurations phase results in implementation of a secure configuration baseline for each information system and constituent CIs, i.e., each established CI is the object of a documented and approved secure configuration.

3.2.1 ESTABLISH SECURE CONFIGURATIONS

In developing and deploying an information system, secure configurations are established for the information system and its constituent CIs. Secure configurations may include:

- Setting secure values (i.e., the parameters that describe how particular automated functions of IT products behave) including, but not limited to:

    o OS and application features (enabling or disabling depending on the specific feature, setting specific parameters, etc.);
    o Services (e.g., automatic updates) and ports (e.g., DNS over port 53);
    o Network protocols (e.g., NetBIOS, IPv6) and network interfaces (e.g., Bluetooth, IEEE 802.11, infrared);
    o Methods of remote access (e.g., SSL, VPN, SSH, IPSEC);
    o Access controls (e.g., controlling permissions to files, directories, registry keys, and restricting user activities such as modifying system logs or installing applications);
    o Management of identifiers/accounts (e.g., changing default account names, determining length of time until inactive accounts are disabled, using unique user names, establishing user groups);
    o Authentication controls (e.g., password length, use of special characters, minimum password age, multifactor authentication/use of tokens);
    o Audit settings (e.g., capturing key events such as failures, logons, permission changes, unsuccessful file access, creation of users and objects, deletion and modification of system files, registry key and kernel changes);
    o System settings (e.g., session timeouts, number of remote connections, session lock); and
    o Cryptography (e.g., using FIPS 140-2-validated cryptographic protocols and algorithms to protect data in transit and in storage);

- Applying vendor-released patches in response to identified vulnerabilities, including software updates;
- Using approved, signed software, if supported;
- Implementing safeguards through software to protect end-user machines against attack (e.g., antivirus, antispyware, antiadware, personal firewalls, host-based intrusion detection systems [HIDS]);
- Applying network protections (e.g., TLS, IPSEC);
- Establishing the location where a component physically and logically resides (e.g., behind a firewall, within a DMZ, on a specific subnet, etc.); and
- Maintaining and updating technical specification and design documentation, system security documentation, system procedures, etc.

In many cases, organizational policies, in accordance with federal laws, standards, directives, and orders, establish generally accepted common secure configurations (e.g., National Checklist

Program, DISA STIGs, CIS benchmarks). Configurations identified in the National Checklist Program[22] as well as SCAP-expressed checklists are a source for establishing common secure configurations. Commercial product developers are also a potential source for common secure configurations. Deviations from common secure configurations are justified and recorded (see Section 3.2.2.iii).

In establishing and maintaining secure configurations, organizations consider potential interoperability conflicts with interconnected systems. Coordination of secure configuration baselines between system staff and/or the relevant CCB(s) helps ensure synchronization of secure configurations between interconnected systems to meet desired security and operational functionality.

If not identified in organizational policies and procedures, the IS owner, in coordination with the ISSO, has the responsibility of establishing secure configurations (based on appropriate common secure configurations, if available) for an information system and its constituent CIs. Regardless of the responsible party, the secure configurations comply with all applicable federal requirements and are approved in accordance with organizational policy.

SDLC Phase: Begin in Development/Acquisition phase, finalize in Implementation/Assessment phase

Primary Roles: ISO; ISSO

Supporting Roles: ISA; System/Software Developer

Expected Input: Organizational and/or system-level policies and procedures including mandated or suggested common secure configurations; System Security Plan/information system security requirements; system/component technical documentation

Expected Output: Initial secure baseline configuration(s) for the information system and its CI(s)

3.2.2 IMPLEMENT SECURE CONFIGURATIONS

Implementing secure configurations for IT products is no simple task. There are many IT products, and each has a myriad of possible parameters that can be configured. In addition, organizations have mission and business process needs which may require that IT products be configured in a particular manner. To further complicate matters, for some products, the configuration settings of the underlying platform may need to be modified to allow for the functionality required for mission accomplishment such that they deviate from the approved common secure configurations.

Using the secure configuration previously established (see Section 3.2.1) as a starting point, the following structured approach is recommended when implementing the secure configuration:

i. Prioritize Configurations

In the ideal environment, all IT products within an organization would be configured to the most secure state that still provided the functionality required by the organization.

---

[22] National Institute of Standards and Technology Special Publication 800-70, *National Checklist Program for IT Products Guidance for Checklists Users and Developers*, as amended, provides information on the National Checklist Program. Also see http://checklists.nist.gov.

However, due to limited resources and other constraints, many organizations may find it necessary to prioritize which information systems, IT products, or CIs to target first for secure configuration as they implement SecCM.

In determining the priorities for implementing secure configurations in information systems, IT products, or CIs, organizations consider the following criteria:

- System impact level – Implementing secure configurations in information systems with a high or moderate security impact level may have priority over information systems with a low security impact level.
- Risk assessments – Risk assessments can be used to target information systems, IT products, or CIs having the most impact on security and organizational risk.
- Vulnerability scanning – Vulnerability scans can be used to target information systems, IT products, or CIs that are most vulnerable. For example, the Common Vulnerability Scoring System (CVSS) is a specification within SCAP that provides an open framework for communicating the characteristics of software flaw vulnerabilities and in calculating their relative severity. CVSS scores can be used to help prioritize configuration and patching activities.
- Degree of penetration – The degree of penetration represents the extent to which the same product is deployed within an information technology environment. For example, if an organization uses a specific operating system on 95 percent of its workstations, it may obtain the most immediate value by planning and deploying secure configurations for that operating system. Other IT products or CIs can be targeted afterwards.

ii. Test Configurations

Organizations fully test secure configurations prior to implementation in the production environment. There are a number of issues that may be encountered when implementing configurations including software compatibility and hardware device driver issues. For example, there may be legacy applications with special operating requirements that do not function correctly after a common secure configuration has been applied. Additionally, configuration errors could occur if OS and multiple application configurations are applied to the same component. For example, a setting for an application configuration parameter may conflict with a similar setting for an OS configuration parameter.

Virtual environments are recommended for testing secure configurations as they allow organizations to examine the functional impact on applications without having to configure actual machines.

iii. Resolve Issues and Document Deviations

Testing secure configuration implementations may introduce functional problems within the system or applications. For example, the new secure configuration may close a port or stop a service that is needed for OS or application functionality. These problems are examined individually and either resolved or documented as a deviation from, or exception to, the established common secure configurations.

In some cases, changing one configuration setting may require changes to another setting, another CI, or another information system. For instance, a common secure configuration may specify strengthened password requirements which may require a change to existing single sign-on applications. Or there may be a requirement that the OS-provided firewall be enabled by default. To ensure that applications function as expected, the firewall policy may need to be revised to allow specific ports, services, IP addresses, etc. When conflicts between applications and secure configurations cannot be resolved, deviations are documented and approved through the configuration change control process as appropriate.

iv. Record and Approve the Baseline Configuration

The established and tested secure configuration, including any necessary deviations, represents the preliminary baseline configuration and is recorded in order to support configuration change control/security impact analysis, incident resolution, problem solving, and monitoring activities. Once recorded, the preliminary baseline configuration is approved in accordance with organizationally defined policy. Once approved, the preliminary baseline configuration becomes the initial baseline configuration for the information system and its constituent CIs.

The baseline configuration of an information system includes the sum total of the secure configurations of its constituent CIs and represents the system-specific configuration against which all changes are controlled.

The baseline configuration may include, as applicable, information regarding the system architecture, the interconnection of hardware components, secure configuration settings of software components, the software load, supporting documentation, and the elements in a release package. There could be a different baseline configuration for each life cycle stage (development, test, staging, production) of the information system.

When possible, organizations employ automated tools to support the management of baseline configurations and to keep the configuration information as up to date and near real time as possible. There are a number of solutions which maintain baseline configurations for a wide variety of hardware and software products. Some comprehensive SecCM solutions integrate the maintenance of baseline configurations with component inventory and monitoring tools.

v. Deploy the Baseline Configuration

Organizations are encouraged to implement baseline configurations in a centralized and automated manner using automated configuration management tools, automated scripts, vendor-provided mechanisms, etc.

Media libraries may be used to store, protect, and control the master copies of approved versions of baseline configurations. Media may be the means to store information (paper, tapes, CD/DVDs, USB drives, etc.) or the information itself (e.g., files, software code). The media library may also include commercially licensed software, custom-developed software, and other artifacts and documents generated throughout the SDLC.

SDLC Phase: Implementation/Assessment phase

Primary Roles: ISO; ISSO

Supporting Roles: ISA; System/Software Developer

Expected Input: Organizational and/or system-level policies and procedures including mandated or suggested common secure configurations; System Security Plan/information system security requirements; system/component technical documentation

Expected Output: Approved, recorded, and deployed secure baseline configuration(s) for system CI(s), including recorded deviations from common secure configurations

3.3 CONTROLLING CONFIGURATION CHANGE

If organizations are to maintain secure configurations for their information systems in an environment where technology is continually evolving and the number and seriousness of threats is expanding, changes to system configurations need to be managed and controlled.

The following subsections describe the *Controlling Configuration Changes* phase activities. In this phase, the activities are normally implemented at the system level following policy and procedures. The following subsections are listed in the order in which the configuration activities typically occur. As always, organizations have flexibility in determining which activities are performed at what level and in what order. Completion of the Controlling Configuration Changes phase results in implementation of access restrictions for change, and documented configuration change control and security impact analysis processes.

3.3.1 IMPLEMENT ACCESS RESTRICTIONS FOR CHANGE

Access restrictions for change represent the enforcement side of SecCM. Configuration change control is a process for funneling changes for an information system through a managed process; however, without access restrictions, there is nothing preventing someone from implementing changes outside of the process. Access restrictions are a mechanism to enforce configuration control processes by controlling who has access to the information system and/or its constituent CIs to make changes. Access restrictions for change may also include controlling access to additional change-related information such as change requests, records, correspondence, change test plans and results, etc.

To implement access restrictions for change:

    i. Determine the possible types of configuration changes that can be made in the information system including network, operating system, and application layers;

    ii. Determine which individuals have privileged access and which of those privileged individuals are authorized to make what types of changes; and

    iii. Implement technical mechanisms (e.g., role-based access, file/group permissions, etc.) to ensure that only authorized individuals are able to make the appropriate changes.

SDLC Phase: Implementation/Assessment phase

Primary Roles: ISO; ISSO

Supporting Roles: ISA

Expected Input: System Security Plan/system security requirements; organizational and/or system-level policies and procedures

Expected Output: Appropriate access restrictions for change implemented for the system

3.3.2   IMPLEMENT THE CONFIGURATION CHANGE CONTROL PROCESS

A well-defined configuration change control process is fundamental to any SecCM program. Configuration change control is the process for ensuring that configuration changes to an information system are formally requested, evaluated for their security impact, tested for effectiveness, and approved before they are implemented. Although the process may have different steps and levels of rigor depending on organizational risk tolerance and/or system-impact level, it generally consists of the following steps:

i.   **Request** the change. A request for change may originate from any number of sources including the end user of the information system, a help desk, or from management. Proposed changes may also originate from vendor-supplied patches, application updates, security alerts, system scans, etc. See Appendix E for a Sample Change Request Template.

ii.   **Record** the request for the proposed change. A change request is formally entered into the configuration change control process when it is recorded in accordance with organizational procedures. Organizations may use paper-based requests, emails, a help desk, and/or automated tools to track change requests, route them based on workflow processes, and allow for electronic acknowledgements/approvals.

iii.   **Determine** if the proposed change requires configuration control. Some types of changes may be exempt from configuration change control or pre-approved as defined in the SecCM plan and/or procedures. If the change is exempt or pre-approved, note this on the change request and allow the change to be made without further analysis or approval; however, system documentation may still require updating (e.g., the System Security Plan, the baseline configuration, IS component inventory, etc.).

iv.   **Analyze** the proposed change for its security impact on the information system (see Section 3.3.3).

v.   **Test** the proposed change for security and functional impacts. Testing confirms the impacts identified during analysis and/or reveals additional impacts. The impacts of the change are presented to the CCB and to the AO.

vi.   **Approve** the change. This step is usually performed by the CCB. The CCB may require the implementation of additional controls if the change is necessary for mission accomplishment but has a negative impact on the security of the system and organization. Implementation of additional controls is coordinated with the AO and ISO.

vii.   **Implement** the approved change. Once approved, authorized staff makes the change. Depending upon the scope of the change, it may be helpful to develop an implementation plan. Change implementation includes changes to applicable/related configuration parameters as well as updating system documentation to reflect the change(s). Stakeholders (e.g., users, management, help desk, etc.) are notified about the change, especially if the change implementation requires a service interruption or alters the functionality of the information system. In the case of the latter situation, user and help desk training may be required.

viii. **Verify** that the change was implemented correctly (e.g., vulnerability scans, post-implementation security and functionality analysis, reassessment of affected security controls, etc.). Configuration change control is not complete and a change request not closed until it has been confirmed that the change was deployed without issues. Although the initial security impact analysis and testing may have found no impact from the change, an improperly implemented change can cause its own security issues.

ix. **Close** out the change request. With completion of the above steps, the change request is closed out in accordance with organizational procedures.

Changes are also evaluated for consistency with organizational enterprise architecture.

If configuration change control procedures have been defined by the organization, the information system owner interprets the procedures in the context of the target information system, and refines the process to make it practical to perform. These changes to the process may need to be approved by the organizational CCB in accordance with SecCM policy.

It is important that IT operations and maintenance staff who support the information system are active participants in the configuration change control process and are aware of their responsibility for following it. If significant business process reengineering is needed, for example, updating help desk activities or a patch management process, training may be required.

Unscheduled or Unauthorized Changes

Unfortunately, it is not uncommon to see activities such as deploying or disposing of hardware, making changes to configurations, and installing patches occurring outside the configuration change control process even though these activities can have a significant impact on the security of an information system. Additionally, situations may arise that necessitate an unscheduled (emergency) change. It is incumbent upon information system owners to identify all sources of change to make certain that changes requiring configuration control go through the configuration change control process, even if it is after the fact.

When unscheduled changes must be made and time does not allow for following the established configuration change control process, unscheduled changes are still managed and controlled. Organizations include instructions for handling unscheduled changes within the configuration change control procedures as well as instructions for handling unauthorized changes that are subsequently discovered. Configuration change control procedures also address flaw remediation to allow rapid but controlled change to fix software errors. Unscheduled changes are reviewed/resolved by the CCB as soon as is practical after unscheduled changes are made.

SDLC Phase: Implementation/Assessment phase, ongoing during the Operations and Maintenance phase

Primary Roles: ISO; CCB; ISSO

Supporting Roles: ISA; User

Expected Input: Organizational and/or system-level SecCM policies and procedures; System Security Plan/system security requirements

Expected Output: Documented and implemented configuration change control process

3.3.3 CONDUCT SECURITY IMPACT ANALYSIS

This is one of the most critical steps in the configuration change control process with respect to SecCM. Organizations spend significant resources developing and maintaining the secure state of information systems; failing to properly analyze a change for its security impact can undo this effort and expose the organization to attack. The security impact analysis activity provides the linkage between configuration change control and improved security. The management of changes through a structured process has its own benefits – for instance, increased efficiency. However, it is only when those changes are evaluated for their security impact that the configuration change control process realizes benefits for the security posture of an information system.

Very large organizations or ISOs of large and complex systems may find it helpful to create a Configuration Review Board to manage and conduct security impact analyses and report the findings to the relevant CCB.

Changes are examined for impact on security, and for mitigating controls that can be implemented to reduce any resulting vulnerability. Security impact analyses are conducted by individuals or teams with technical knowledge of the information system throughout the SDLC such that the impact of changes on security is considered at every phase:[23]

- **Initiation Phase (Before a Change is Deployed)**
  Security impact analysis before a change is deployed is critical in ascertaining whether the change will impact the secure state of the information system. The initial security impact analysis is conducted before the change is approved by the CCB. If there are security concerns with a change, they can be addressed/mitigated before time and energy are spent in building, testing, and/or rolling out the change.

- **Development/Acquisition and Implementation/Assessment Phases**
  Security impact analysis is not a one-time event conducted during the initiation phase to support the decisions of the CCB when approving changes. When the change is initially proposed and reviewed, the manner in which it will be built and implemented may not be known, something which can greatly influence the security impact of the change. For instance, for a custom-built component during the design phase, security impact analysis is performed on technical design documents to ensure that the design considers security best practices, implements the appropriate controls, and would not need to be redeveloped at a later date due to introduced vulnerabilities. Developers ensure that security is taken into account as they build the component, and the design is tested during implementation to confirm that expected controls were implemented and that no new or unexpected vulnerabilities were introduced.

- **Operations and Maintenance Phase (After a Change is Deployed)** – This confirms that the original security impact analysis was correct, and that unexpected vulnerabilities or impacts to security controls not identified in the testing environment have not been introduced. Additionally, the security impact of unscheduled and unauthorized changes is analyzed during the operations and maintenance phase.

---

[23] Review NIST SP 800-27 and SP 800-64 for guidance on integrating security into the SDLC.

The process for a security impact analysis consists of the following steps:

i. **Understand the Change** - If the change is being proposed, develop a high-level architecture overview which shows how the change will be implemented. If the change has already occurred (unscheduled/unauthorized), request follow-up documentation/information and review it or use whatever information is available (e.g., audit records, interview staff who made the change, etc.) to gain insight into the change.

ii. **Identify Vulnerabilities** - If the change involves a COTS hardware or software product, identifying vulnerabilities may include, for example, a search of the National Vulnerability Database (NVD)[24] which enumerates vulnerabilities, user experience, etc. Organizations can leverage this information to address known issues and remove or mitigate them before they become a concern. Other public databases of vulnerabilities, weaknesses, and threats may also be searched (e.g., US-CERT). Some automated vulnerability scanning tools (SCAP-validated tools where possible) are able to search various public vulnerability databases that apply to IT products/CPE names of IT products. If the change involves custom development, a more in-depth analysis of the security impact is conducted. Although application security is beyond the scope of this publication, there are many best practices and useful sources of information for how to ensure the security of software code.

iii. **Assess Risks** - Once a vulnerability has been identified, a risk assessment is needed to identify the likelihood of a threat exercising the vulnerability and the impact of such an event. Although vulnerabilities may be identified in changes as they are proposed, built, and tested, the assessed risk may be low enough that the risk can be accepted without remediation (i.e., risk acceptance). In other cases, the risk may be high enough that the change is not approved (i.e., risk avoidance), or that safeguards and countermeasures are implemented to reduce the risk (i.e., risk mitigation).[25]

iv. **Assess Impact on Existing Security Controls** - In addition to assessing the risk from the change, organizations analyze whether and how a change will impact existing security controls. For example, the change may involve installation of software that alters the existing baseline configuration, or the change itself may cause or require changes to the existing baseline configuration. The change may also affect other systems or system components that depend on the function or component being changed, either temporarily or permanently. For example, if a database that is used to support auditing controls is being upgraded to the latest version, auditing functionality within the system may be halted while the upgrade is being implemented.

v. **Plan Safeguards and Countermeasures** - In cases where risks have been identified and are unacceptable, organizations use the security impact analysis to revise the change or to plan safeguards and countermeasures to reduce the risk. For instance, if the security impact analysis reveals that the proposed change causes a modification to a common secure configuration setting, plans to rework the change to function within the existing setting are initiated. If a change involves new elevated privileges for users, plans to mitigate the additional risk are made (e.g., submission of requests for higher clearance levels for those users or implementation of stronger access controls).

---

[24] http://nvd.nist.gov/

[25] See NIST SP 800-30 as amended for more information on risk assessment.

See Appendix I for a sample Security Impact Analysis Template.

SDLC Phase: Operations and Maintenance phase

Primary Roles: ISSO

Supporting Roles: AO; ISO; ISA; System/Software Developer

Expected Input: Change request and/or any supporting documentation; System Security Plan including the current approved baseline configuration; system audit records; relevant COTS vulnerability information

Expected Output: Identified vulnerabilities; risk assessment of identified vulnerabilities including any potential countermeasures; analysis of the security impact of the change

3.3.4 RECORD AND ARCHIVE

Once the change has been analyzed, approved, tested, implemented, and verified, the organization ensures that updates have been made to supporting documents such as technical designs and baseline configurations, in addition to security-related documentation such as System Security Plans, Risk Assessments, Security Assessment Reports, and Plans of Action & Milestones. In cases where there is high risk or where significant changes have been made, a system reauthorization may be required.

As changes are made to baseline configurations, the new baseline becomes the current version, and the previous baseline is no longer valid but is retained for historical purposes. If there are issues with a production release, retention of previous versions allows for a rollback or restoration to a previous secure and functional version of the baseline configuration. Additionally, archiving previous baseline configurations is useful for incident response and traceability support during formal audits.[26]

SDLC Phase: Operations and Maintenance phase

Primary Roles: ISSO

Supporting Roles: ISO; ISA; System/Software Developer

Expected Input: Identified vulnerabilities; risk assessment of identified vulnerabilities including any potential countermeasures; analysis of the security impact of the change

Expected Output: Updated technical and system security-related documentation; decision on whether or not a system reauthorization is required; new baseline configuration

3.4 SECCM MONITORING

If an information system is inconsistent with approved configurations as defined by the organization's baseline configurations of system CIs, the System Security Plan, etc., or an organization's component inventory is inaccurate, the organization may be unaware of potential vulnerabilities and not take actions that would otherwise limit those vulnerabilities and protect it

---

[26] Archived baselines are protected in accordance with the system impact level.

from attacks. Monitoring activities offer the organization better visibility into the actual state of security for its information systems and also support adherence to SecCM policies and procedures. SecCM monitoring also provides input to the organization's overall continuous monitoring strategy.[27]

Organizations implement the configuration monitoring strategy developed during the SecCM planning phase. SecCM monitoring activities confirm that the existing configuration is identical to the current approved baseline configuration, that all items in the component inventory can be identified and are associated with the appropriate information system, and, if possible, whether there are any unapproved (i.e., not recorded in the component inventory) components. Unapproved components are often a major threat to security; they rarely have updated patches, are not configured using the approved baseline configurations, and are not assessed or included in the authorization to operate. For example, if a technician uses a router for testing and then forgets to remove it, or if an employee sets up a wireless access point in a remote office without management consent, the organization may be vulnerable without being aware of it.

3.4.1   ASSESSMENT AND REPORTING

SecCM monitoring is accomplished through assessment and reporting activities. For organizations with a large number of components, the only practical and effective solution for SecCM monitoring activities is the use of automated solutions that use standardized reporting methods such as SCAP. An information system may have many components and many baseline configurations. To manually collect information on the configuration of all components and assess them against policy and approved baseline configurations is not practical, or even possible, in most cases. Automated tools can also facilitate reporting for Security Information and Event Management applications that can be accessed by management and/or formatted into other reports on baseline configuration status. Care is exercised in collecting and analyzing the results generated by automated tools to account for any false positives.

SecCM monitoring may be supported by numerous means, including, but not limited to:

- Scanning to discover components not recorded in the inventory. For example, after testing of a new firewall, a technician forgets to remove it from the network. If it is not properly configured, it may provide access to the network for intruders. A scan would identify this network device as not a part of the inventory, enabling the organization to take action.

- Scanning to identify disparities between the approved baseline configuration and the actual configuration for an information system. For example, a technician rolls out a new patch but forgets to update the baseline configurations of the information systems impacted by the new patch. A scan would identify a difference between the actual environment and the description in the baseline configuration enabling the organization to take action. In another example, a new tool is installed on the workstations of a few end users of the information system. During installation, the tool changes a number of configuration settings in the browser on the users' workstations, exposing them to attack. A scan would identify the change in the workstation configuration, allowing the appropriate individuals to take action.

---

[27] See NIST SP 800-37 and NIST SP 800-137.

- Implementation of automated change monitoring tools (e.g., change/configuration management tools, application whitelisting tools). Unauthorized changes to information systems may be an indication that the systems are under attack or that SecCM procedures are not being followed or need updating. Automated tools are available that monitor information systems for changes and alert system staff if unauthorized changes occur or are attempted.

- Querying audit records/log monitoring to identify unauthorized change events.

- Running system integrity checks to verify that baseline configurations have not been changed.

- Reviewing configuration change control records (including system impact analyses) to verify conformance with SecCM policy and procedures.

When possible, organizations seek to normalize data to describe their information system in order that the various outputs from monitoring can be combined, correlated, analyzed, and reported in a consistent manner. SCAP provides a common language for describing vulnerabilities, misconfigurations, and products and is an obvious starting point for organizations seeking a consistent way of communicating across the organization regarding the security status of the enterprise architecture (see Section 3.5).

When inconsistencies are discovered as a result of monitoring activities, the organization may want to take remedial action. Action taken may be via manual methods or via use of automated tools. Automated tools are preferable since actions are not reliant upon human intervention and are taken immediately once an unauthorized change is identified. Examples of possible actions include:

- Implementing nondestructive remediation actions (e.g., quarantining of unregistered device(s), blocking insecure protocols, etc.);
- Sending an alert with change details to appropriate staff using email;
- Rolling back changes and restoring from backups;
- Updating the inventory to include newly identified components; and
- Updating baseline configurations to represent new configurations.

Changes detected as a result of monitoring activities are reconciled with approved changes. Specifically, reconciliation attempts to answer the following:

- Who made the change;
- Whether the change occurred in a scheduled maintenance window;
- Whether the change matches a previously detected and approved change; and
- Whether the change corresponds with an approved change request, help desk ticket, or product release.

Additionally, the results of monitoring activities are analyzed to determine the reason(s) that an unauthorized change occurred. There are many potential causes for unauthorized changes. They may stem from:

- Accidental or unintentional changes;
- Malicious intent/attacks;

- Individuals who believe configuration change control processes don't apply to them;
- Individuals who aren't aware of the configuration change control process;
- Errors made when changes are implemented; and
- A delay between introducing the change and updating the inventory and baseline configuration for the affected information systems;

Analyzing unauthorized changes identified through monitoring can not only identify vulnerabilities, but can also give organizations insight into any potential systemic problems with how the configuration change control process is managed. Once organizations are aware of any such problems, they can take actions such as reengineering processes, implementing improved access restrictions for change, and providing training on SecCM processes.

Finally, monitoring may support the generation of metrics related to SecCM activities. Analysis and consolidation of monitoring reports can generate metrics such as the percentage of information systems that are implemented in accordance with their approved baselines, the percentage of IT products that are configured in accordance with the organizationally defined common secure configurations, or percentage of information system changes that have been subjected to security impact analyses. Thus, SecCM monitoring may also be a source of information that supports metrics requirements associated with the organization's overall continuous monitoring process.

Results of SecCM monitoring are reported to management as defined by organizational policy and the SecCM strategy. Various types of reporting may be needed to support compliance with applicable federal laws, Executive Orders, directives, policies, regulations, standards and guidelines.

The SecCM monitoring strategy and procedures are reviewed and revised to ensure that organizational security requirements continue to be met.

SDLC Phase: Operations and Maintenance phase

Primary Roles: SISO (for implementing organization-wide monitoring tools and overseeing monitoring activities potentially including engaging independent assessment teams); ISO (for ensuring that configuration monitoring is implemented at the system level as defined in the strategy)

Supporting Roles: ISSO; ISA; System/Software Developer

Expected Input: SecCM monitoring strategy; automated tools; IS component inventory; current baseline configuration(s); audit records; System Security Plan/system security requirements

Expected Output: SecCM monitoring reports, including security assessment reports and output from automated tools, as defined in the strategy and schedule

3.4.2 IMPLEMENT AND MANAGE TOOLS FOR SECCM MONITORING

SecCM monitoring tools identified during the planning phase are implemented and managed during the monitoring phase. Some tools may support SecCM activities in multiple phases, i.e., tools may have already been implemented and supporting activities during the identifying and implementing configurations phase and/or the controlling configuration changes phase. The monitoring-related functionality of such tools is then leveraged and managed during the monitoring phase.

Before implementing automated monitoring tools, organizations conduct a security impact analysis to ensure that the tools do not have a negative effect on the existing enterprise architecture as a whole or on individual information systems/components.

It is important to note that automated tools may not support or be able to function with all organizational systems or all components within a system. Organizations document the systems and/or components that are not monitored via automated tools and a manual process is developed and implemented for those systems/components.

SDLC Phase: Implementation phase

Primary Roles: SecCM Program Manager; ISO

Supporting Roles: SISO (if s/he is not the SecCM Program Manager); CIO; AO; ISSO; ISA; System/Software Developer

Expected Input: Configuration monitoring strategy; enterprise architecture information and/or system architecture information; tools identified during the planning phase, information about other IT products with which monitoring tools will interface

Expected Output: Implemented configuration monitoring tools

3.5 USING SECURITY CONTENT AUTOMATION PROTOCOL (SCAP)[28]

SCAP is a protocol currently consisting of a suite of specifications[29] that standardize the format and nomenclature by which security software communicates information about software flaws and secure configurations. SCAP-enabled tools can be used for maintaining the security of enterprise systems, such as automatically verifying the installation of patches, checking system security configuration settings, and examining systems for signs of compromise.

To automate configuration management and produce assessment evidence for many NIST SP 800-53 controls, federal agencies use SCAP-enabled tools along with SCAP-expressed checklists. SCAP-expressed checklists are customized as appropriate to meet specific organizational requirements. SCAP-expressed checklists can map individual system configuration settings to their corresponding high-level security requirements. These mappings can help demonstrate that the implemented settings adhere to requirements. The mappings are embedded in SCAP-expressed checklists which allow SCAP-enabled tools to automatically generate standardized assessment and compliance evidence. This can provide a substantial savings in effort and cost. If SCAP-enabled tools are not available or are not currently deployed within an organization, organizations plan ahead by implementing SCAP-expressed checklists for their common secure configurations in order to be well positioned when SCAP-enabled tools become available and/or are deployed.

---

[28] National Institute of Standards and Technology Special Publication 800-117, *Guide to Adopting and Using the Security Content Automation Protocol* and 800-126, *The Technical Specification for the Security Content Automation Protocol* provide information on the Security Content Automation Protocol. The text in Section 3.5 was taken from NIST SP 800-117, pages ES-1 and ES-2.

[29] Additional SCAP specifications are expected to be added, check http://scap.nist.gov/ for updates.

Organizations encourage security software vendors to incorporate support for Common Vulnerabilities and Exposures (CVE), Common Configuration Enumeration (CCE), and Common Platform Enumeration (CPE) into their products, as well as encourage all software vendors to include CVE and CCE identifiers and CPE product names in their vulnerability and patch advisories.

SCAP Version 1.2 Components[30]

SCAP Component	Description	Maintaining Organization
Enumerations		
Common Configuration Enumeration (CCE)	Nomenclature and dictionary of system security issues	MITRE Corporation
Common Platform Enumeration (CPE)	Nomenclature and dictionary of product names and versions	MITRE Corporation
Common Vulnerabilities and Exposures (CVE)	Nomenclature and dictionary of security-related software flaws	MITRE Corporation
Vulnerability Measurement and Scoring		
Common Vulnerability Scoring System (CVSS)	Specification for measuring the relative severity of software flaw vulnerabilities	Forum of Incident Response and Security Teams (FIRST)
Common Configuration Scoring System (CCSS)	Specification for measuring the severity of software security configuration issues	NIST
Expression and Checking Languages		
Extensible Configuration Checklist Description Format (XCCDF)	Language for specifying checklists and reporting checklist results	National Security Agency (NSA) and NIST
Open Vulnerability and Assessment Language (OVAL)	Language for specifying low-level testing procedures used by checklists	MITRE Corporation
Open Checklist Interactive Language (OCIL)	Language for expressing security checks that cannot be evaluated without some human interaction or feedback.	MITRE Corporation
Asset Reporting Format (ARF)	A data model for expressing the transport format of information about assets and the relationships between assets and reports	NIST
Asset Identification	Constructs to uniquely identify assets based on known identifiers and/or known information about the assets	MITRE Corporation and NIST

---

[30] Table taken from National Institute of Standards and Technology Special Publication 800-117. The OCIL, CCSS, ARF and Asset Identification information was added based on NIST SP 800-126r2. Additional SCAP specifications are expected to be added, check http://scap.nist.gov/revision/ for updates.

APPENDIX A

REFERENCES

LAWS, POLICIES, DIRECTIVES, REGULATIONS, MEMORANDA, STANDARDS, AND GUIDELINES

LEGISLATION

1. E-Government Act [includes FISMA] (P.L. 107-347), December 2002.

2. Federal Information Security Management Act (P.L. 107-347, Title III), December 2002.

3. Paperwork Reduction Act (P.L. 104-13), May 1995.

POLICIES, DIRECTIVES, INSTRUCTIONS, AND MEMORANDA

4. Office of Management and Budget, Federal Enterprise Architecture Program Management Office, *FEA Consolidated Reference Model Document*, Version 2.3, October 2007.

5. Office of Management and Budget, *Federal Segment Architecture Methodology (FSAM)*, January 2009.

6. Office of Management and Budget Memorandum M-07-11, *Implementation of Commonly Accepted Security Configurations for Windows Operating Systems*, March 2007.

7. Office of Management and Budget Memorandum M-07-18, *Ensuring New Acquisitions Include Common Security Configurations*, June 2007.

8. Office of Management and Budget Memorandum M-08-22, *Guidance on the Federal Desktop Core Configuration (FDCC)*, August 2008.

9. Office of Management and Budget Memorandum M-10-15, *FY 2010 Reporting Instructions for the Federal Information Security Management Act and Agency Privacy Management*, April 2010.

10. Committee for National Security Systems (CNSS) Instruction 4009, *National Information Assurance (IA) Glossary*, April 2010.

STANDARDS

11. IEEE SA - 828-2005, *IEEE Standard for Software Configuration Management Plans*, http://standards.ieee.org/findstds/standard/828-2005 html.

12. International Organization for Standardization (ISO) 10007:2003, *Quality management systems – Guidelines for configuration management*, (http://www.iso.org/iso/catalogue_detail htm?csnumber=36644).

13. International Organization for Standardization (ISO) ISO/ IEC 21827:2008 Information technology - Security techniques - Systems Security Engineering - Capability Maturity Model® (SSE-CMM®), (http://www.iso.org/iso/iso_catalogue/catalogue_ics/catalogue_detail_ics htm?csnumber=44716).

14. National Institute of Standards and Technology Federal Information Processing Standards Publication 140-2, *Security Requirements for Cryptographic Modules*, May 2001.

15. National Institute of Standards and Technology Federal Information Processing Standards Publication 199, *Standards for Security Categorization of Federal Information and Information Systems*, February 2004.

16. National Institute of Standards and Technology Federal Information Processing Standards Publication 200, *Minimum Security Requirements for Federal Information and Information Systems,* March 2006.

GUIDELINES

17. National Institute of Standards and Technology Special Publication 800-16, (Draft) *Information Technology Security Training Requirements: A Role- and Performance-Based Model*, March 2009.

18. National Institute of Standards and Technology Special Publication 800-18, Revision 1, *Guide for Developing Security Plans for Federal Information Systems*, February 2006.

19. National Institute of Standards and Technology Special Publication 800-21, 2nd Edition, *Guideline for Implementing Cryptography in the Federal Government*, December 2005.

20. National Institute of Standards and Technology Special Publication 800-24, *PBX Vulnerability Analysis: Finding Holes in Your PBX Before Someone Else Does*, August 2000.

21. National Institute of Standards and Technology Special Publication 800-25, *Federal Agency Use of Public Key Technology for Digital Signatures and Authentication*, October 2000.

22. National Institute of Standards and Technology Special Publication 800-27, Revision A, *Engineering Principles for Information Technology Security (A Baseline for Achieving Security)*, June 2004.

23. National Institute of Standards and Technology Special Publication 800-28, Version 2, *Guidelines on Active Content and Mobile Code*, March 2008.

24. National Institute of Standards and Technology Special Publication 800-29, *A Comparison of the Security Requirements for Cryptographic Modules in FIPS 140-1 and FIPS 140-2*, June 2001.

25. National Institute of Standards and Technology Special Publication 800-30 Revision 1, *Guide for Conducting Risk Assessments*, (Projected Publication Summer 2011).

26. National Institute of Standards and Technology Special Publication 800-32, *Introduction to Public Key Technology and the Federal PKI Infrastructure*, February 2001.

27. National Institute of Standards and Technology Special Publication 800-37, Revision 1, *Guide for Applying the Risk Management Framework to Federal Information Systems: A Security Life Cycle Approach*, February 2010.

28. National Institute of Standards and Technology Special Publication 800-39, *Managing Information Security Risk: Organization, Mission, and Information System View*, March 2011.

29. National Institute of Standards and Technology Special Publication 800-40, Version 2.0, *Creating a Patch and Vulnerability Management Program*, November 2005.

30. National Institute of Standards and Technology Special Publication 800-41, Revision 1, *Guidelines on Firewalls and Firewall Policy*, September 2009.

31. National Institute of Standards and Technology Special Publication 800-44, Version 2, *Guidelines on Securing Public Web Servers*, September 2007.

32. National Institute of Standards and Technology Special Publication 800-45, Version 2, *Guidelines on Electronic Mail Security*, February 2007.

33. National Institute of Standards and Technology Special Publication 800-46, Revision 1, *Guide to Enterprise Telework and Remote Access Security*, June 2009.

34. National Institute of Standards and Technology Special Publication 800-47, *Security Guide for Interconnecting Information Technology Systems*, August 2002.

35. National Institute of Standards and Technology Special Publication 800-48, Revision 1, *Guide to Securing Legacy IEEE 802.11 Wireless Networks*, July 2008.

36. National Institute of Standards and Technology Special Publication 800-51, Revision 1, *Guide to Using Vulnerability Naming Schemes*, February 2011.

37. National Institute of Standards and Technology Special Publication 800-52, *Guidelines for the Selection and Use of Transport Layer Security (TLS) Implementations*, June 2005.

38. National Institute of Standards and Technology Special Publication 800-53, Revision 3, *Recommended Security Controls for Federal Information Systems and Organizations*, August 2009.

39. National Institute of Standards and Technology Special Publication 800-53A, Revision 1, *Guide for Assessing the Security Controls in Federal Information Systems* and Organizations, June 2010.

40. National Institute of Standards and Technology Special Publication 800-54, *Border Gateway Protocol Security*, July 2007.

41. National Institute of Standards and Technology Special Publication 800-55, Revision 1, *Performance Measurement Guide for Information Security*, July 2008.

42. National Institute of Standards and Technology Special Publication 800-57, *Recommendation for Key Management Part 1: General*, Draft May 2011.

43. National Institute of Standards and Technology Special Publication 800-57, Part 3, *Recommendation for Key Management Part 3, Application-Specific Key Management Guidance*, December 2009.

44. National Institute of Standards and Technology Special Publication 800-58, *Security Considerations for Voice Over IP Systems*, January 2005.

45. National Institute of Standards and Technology Special Publication 800-63, Revision 1, (Draft), *Electronic Authentication Guidance*, December 2008.

46. National Institute of Standards and Technology Special Publication 800-64, Revision 2, *Security Considerations in the System Development Life Cycle*, October 2008.

47. National Institute of Standards and Technology Special Publication 800-68 Revision 1, *Guidance for Securing Microsoft Windows XP Systems for IT Professionals*, October 2008.

48. National Institute of Standards and Technology Special Publication 800-69, *Guidance for Securing Microsoft Windows XP Home Edition: A NIST Security Configuration Checklist*, September 2006.

49. National Institute of Standards and Technology Special Publication 800-70, Revision 2, *National Checklist Program for IT Products: Guidelines for Checklist Users and Developers*, February 2011.

50. National Institute of Standards and Technology Special Publication 800-77, *Guide to IPSec VPNs*, December 2005.

51. National Institute of Standards and Technology Special Publication 800-81, Revision 1 *Secure Domain Name System (DNS) Deployment Guide,* April 2010.

52. National Institute of Standards and Technology Special Publication 800-82, *Guide to Industrial Control Systems (ICS) Security,* June 2011.

53. National Institute of Standards and Technology Special Publication 800-92, *Guide to Computer Security Log Management*, September 2006.

54. National Institute of Standards and Technology Special Publication 800-94, *Guide to Intrusion Detection and Prevention Systems (IDPS)*, February 2007.

55. National Institute of Standards and Technology Special Publication 800-95, *Guide to Secure Web Services*, August 2007.

56. National Institute of Standards and Technology Special Publication 800-97, *Establishing Wireless Robust Security Networks: A Guide to IEEE 802.11i*, February 2007.

57. National Institute of Standards and Technology Special Publication 800-98, *Guidelines for Security Radio Frequency Identification (RFID) Systems*, April 2007.

58. National Institute of Standards and Technology Special Publication 800-100, *Information Security Handbook: A Guide for Managers*, October 2006.

59. National Institute of Standards and Technology Special Publication 800-107, *Recommendation for Applications Using Approved Hash Algorithms*, February 2009.

60. National Institute of Standards and Technology Special Publication 800-111, *Guide to Storage Encryption Technologies for End User Devices,* November 2007.

61. National Institute of Standards and Technology Special Publication 800-113, *Guide to SSL VPNs,* July 2008.

62. National Institute of Standards and Technology Special Publication 800-115, *Technical Guide to Information Security Testing and Assessment*, September 2008.

63. National Institute of Standards and Technology Special Publication 800-117, *Guide to Adopting and Using the Security Content Automation Protocol (SCAP)*, July 2010

64. National Institute of Standards and Technology Special Publication 800-118, *Guide to Enterprise Password Management* (Draft), April 2009.

65. National Institute of Standards and Technology Special Publication 800-121, *Guide to Bluetooth Security*, September 2008.

66. National Institute of Standards and Technology Special Publication 800-122, *Guide to Protecting the Confidentiality of Personally Identifiable Information (PII)*, April 2010.

67. National Institute of Standards and Technology Special Publication 800-123, *Guide to General Server Security*, July 2008.

68. National Institute of Standards and Technology Special Publication 800-124, *Guidelines on Cell Phone and PDA Security*, October 2008.

69. National Institute of Standards and Technology Special Publication 800-126, Revision 2, *The Technical Specification for the Security Content Automation Protocol (SCAP): SCAP Version 1.2* (Draft), July 2011.

70. National Institute of Standards and Technology Special Publication 800-130, *A Framework for Designing Cryptographic Key Management Systems* (Draft), June 2010.

71. National Institute of Standards and Technology Special Publication 800-131A, *Transitions Recommendation for Transitioning the Use of Cryptographic Algorithms and Key Lengths*, January 2011.

72. National Institute of Standards and Technology Special Publication 800-132, *Recommendation for Password-Based Key Derivation Part 1: Storage Applications*, December 2010.

73. National Institute of Standards and Technology Special Publication 800-135, *Recommendation for Existing Application-Specific Key Derivation Functions*, December 2010.

74. National Institute of Standards and Technology Special Publication 800-137, *Information Security Continuous Monitoring for Federal Information Systems and Organizations* (Draft), December 2010.

MISCELLANEOUS PUBLICATIONS

75. Capability Maturity Model Integration (CMMI) (http://www.sei.cmu.edu/cmmi/).

76. Information Technology Infrastructure Library (ITIL) (http://www.itil-officialsite.com/home/home.asp).

77. National Institute of Standards and Technology Interagency Report 7275, Revision 4, *Specification for the Extensible Configuration Checklist Description Format (XCCDF) Version 1.2* (Draft), July 2010.

78. National Institute of Standards and Technology Interagency Report 7435, *The Common Vulnerability Scoring System (CVSS) and its Applicability to Federal Agency Systems*, August 2007.

79. National Institute of Standards and Technology Interagency Report 7502, *The Common Configuration Scoring System (CCSS): Metrics for Software Security Configuration Vulnerabilities*, December 2010.

80. National Institute of Standards and Technology Interagency Report 7692, *Specification for the Open Checklist Interactive Language (OCIL), Version 2.0*, April 2011.

81. National Institute of Standards and Technology Interagency Report 7693, *Specification for Asset Identification 1.1*, June 2011.

82. National Institute of Standards and Technology Interagency Report 7694, *Specification for the Asset Reporting Format 1.1*, June 2011.

83. National Institute of Standards and Technology Interagency Report 7695, *Common Platform Enumeration: Naming Specification Version 2.3*, (Draft), April 2011.

84. National Institute of Standards and Technology Interagency Report 7696, *Common Platform Enumeration: Name Matching Specification Version 2.3* (Draft), April 2011.

85. National Institute of Standards and Technology Interagency Report 7697, *Common Platform Enumeration: Dictionary Specification Version 2.3* (Draft), June 2011.

86. National Institute of Standards and Technology Interagency Report 7698, *Common Platform Enumeration: Applicability Language Specification Version 2.3* (Draft), June 2011.

APPENDIX B

GLOSSARY

COMMON TERMS AND DEFINITIONS

Appendix B provides definitions for security terminology used within Special Publication 800-53. Unless specifically defined in this glossary, all terms used in this publication are consistent with those definitions and the definitions contained in CNSS Instruction No. 4009, *National Information Assurance (IA) Glossary.*

Adequate Security [OMB Circular A-130, Appendix III]	Security commensurate with the risk and the magnitude of harm resulting from the loss, misuse, or unauthorized access to or modification of information.
Agency	See Executive Agency.
Asset Identification	SCAP constructs to uniquely identify assets (components) based on known identifiers and/or known information about the assets.
Asset Reporting Format (ARF)	SCAP data model for expressing the transport format of information about assets (components) and the relationships between assets and reports.
Authentication [FIPS 200]	Verifying the identity of a user, process, or device, often as a prerequisite to allowing access to resources in an information system.
Authorizing Official [CNSSI-4009]	A senior (federal) official or executive with the authority to formally assume responsibility for operating an information system at an acceptable level of risk to organizational operations (including mission, functions, image, or reputation), organizational assets, individuals, other organizations, and the Nation.
Baseline Configuration	A set of specifications for a system, or Configuration Item (CI) within a system, that has been formally reviewed and agreed on at a given point in time, and which can be changed only through change control procedures. The baseline configuration is used as a basis for future builds, releases, and/or changes.
Checksum [CNSSI-4009]	A value computed on data to detect error or manipulation.
Chief Information Officer [PL 104-106, Sec. 5125(b)]	Agency official responsible for: (i) Providing advice and other assistance to the head of the executive agency and other senior management personnel of the agency to ensure that information technology is acquired and information resources are managed in a manner that is consistent with laws, Executive Orders, directives, policies, regulations, and priorities established by the head of the agency; (ii) Developing, maintaining, and facilitating the implementation of a sound and integrated information technology architecture for the agency; and (iii) Promoting the effective and efficient design and operation of all major information resources management processes for the agency, including improvements to work processes of the agency.

Common Configuration Enumeration (CCE)	A SCAP specification that provides unique, common identifiers for configuration settings found in a wide variety of hardware and software products.
Common Configuration Scoring System (CCSS)	A SCAP specification for measuring the severity of software security configuration issues.
Common Platform Enumeration (CPE)	A SCAP specification that provides a standard naming convention for operating systems, hardware, and applications for the purpose of providing consistent, easily parsed names that can be shared by multiple parties and solutions to refer to the same specific platform type.[31]
Common Secure Configuration	A recognized standardized and established benchmark (e.g., National Checklist Program, DISA STIGs, CIS Benchmarks, etc.) that stipulates specific secure configuration settings for a given IT platform.
Common Vulnerabilities and Exposures (CVE)	An SCAP specification that provides unique, common names for publicly known information system vulnerabilities.
Common Vulnerability Scoring System (CVSS)	An SCAP specification for communicating the characteristics of vulnerabilities and measuring their relative severity.
Component	See Information System Component.
Configuration	The possible conditions, parameters, and specifications with which an information system or system component can be described or arranged.
Configuration Baseline	See Baseline Configuration.
Configuration Control [CNSSI-4009]	Process for controlling modifications to hardware, firmware, software, and documentation to protect the information system against improper modifications before, during, and after system implementation.
Configuration Control Board [CNSSI-4009]	A group of qualified people with responsibility for the process of regulating and approving changes to hardware, firmware, software, and documentation throughout the development and operational life cycle of an information system.
Configuration Item	An aggregation of information system components that is designated for configuration management and treated as a single entity in the configuration management process.
Configuration Management	A collection of activities focused on establishing and maintaining the integrity of products and systems, through control of the processes for initializing, changing, and monitoring the configurations of those products and systems throughout the system development life cycle.
Configuration Management Plan	A comprehensive description of the roles, responsibilities, policies, and procedures that apply when managing the configuration of products and systems.

---

[31] The MITRE Corporation maintains the CPE specifications and NIST maintains the official CPE Dictionary. More information on CPE is available at http://cpe.mitre.org/. The Official CPE Dictionary is available at http://nvd.nist.gov/cpe.cfm .

Configuration Settings	The set of parameters that can be changed in hardware, software, and/or firmware that affect the security posture and/or functionality of the information system.
End-point Protection Platform	Safeguards implemented through software to protect end-user machines such as workstations and laptops against attack (e.g., antivirus, antispyware, antiadware, personal firewalls, host-based intrusion detection and prevention systems, etc.).
Enterprise Architecture [CNSSI-4009]	The description of an enterprise's entire set of information systems: how they are configured, how they are integrated, how they interface to the external environment at the enterprise's boundary, how they are operated to support the enterprise mission, and how they contribute to the enterprise's overall security posture.
Executive Agency [41 U.S.C., Sec. 403]	An executive Department specified in 5 U.S.C., Sec. 101; a military department specified in 5 U.S.C., Sec. 102; an independent establishment as defined in 5 U.S.C., Sec. 104(1); and a wholly owned Government corporation fully subject to the provisions of 31 U.S.C., Chapter 91.
Extensible Configuration Checklist Description Format (XCCDF)	SCAP language for specifying checklists and reporting checklist results.
Federal Desktop Core Configuration (FDCC)	OMB-mandated set of security configurations for all federal workstation and laptop devices that run either Windows XP or Vista.
Federal Information System [40 U.S.C., Sec. 11331]	An information system used or operated by an executive agency, by a contractor of an executive agency, or by another organization on behalf of an executive agency.
Host-Based Intrusion Detection and Prevention System [SP 800-94]	A program that monitors the characteristics of a single host and the events occurring within that host to identify and stop suspicious activity.
Incident [FIPS 200]	An occurrence that actually or potentially jeopardizes the confidentiality, integrity, or availability of an information system or the information the system processes, stores, or transmits or that constitutes a violation or imminent threat of violation of security policies, security procedures, or acceptable use policies.
Information Resources [44 U.S.C., Sec. 3502]	Information and related resources, such as personnel, equipment, funds, and information technology.
Information Security [44 U.S.C., Sec. 3542]	The protection of information and information systems from unauthorized access, use, disclosure, disruption, modification, or destruction in order to provide confidentiality, integrity, and availability.
Information Security Policy [CNSSI 4009]	Aggregate of directives, regulations, rules, and practices that prescribes how an organization manages, protects, and distributes information.

Information System [44 U.S.C., Sec. 3502]	A discrete set of information resources organized for the collection, processing, maintenance, use, sharing, dissemination, or disposition of information. [Note: Information systems also include specialized systems such as industrial/process controls systems, telephone switching and private branch exchange (PBX) systems, and environmental control systems.]
Information System Administrator	Individual who implements approved secure baseline configurations, incorporates secure configuration settings for IT products, and conducts/assists with configuration monitoring activities as needed.
Information System Component	A discrete identifiable IT asset that represents a building block of an information system.
Information System Component Inventory	A descriptive record of components within an information system.
Information System Owner (or Program Manager) [NIST SP 800-53]	Official responsible for the overall procurement, development, integration, modification, or operation and maintenance of an information system.
Information System Security Officer [NIST SP 800-53]	Individual assigned responsibility for maintaining the appropriate operational security posture for an information system or program. [Note: ISSO responsibility may be assigned by the senior agency information security officer, authorizing official, management official, or information system owner.]
Information System User [CNSSI-4009]	Individual, or (system) process acting on behalf of an individual, authorized to access an information system. [Note: With respect to SecCM, an information system user is an individual who uses the information system functions, initiates change requests, and assists with functional testing.]
Information Technology [40 U.S.C., Sec. 1401]	Any equipment or interconnected system or subsystem of equipment that is used in the automatic acquisition, storage, manipulation, management, movement, control, display, switching, interchange, transmission, or reception of data or information by the executive agency. For purposes of the preceding sentence, equipment is used by an executive agency if the equipment is used by the executive agency directly or is used by a contractor under a contract with the executive agency which: (i) requires the use of such equipment; or (ii) requires the use, to a significant extent, of such equipment in the performance of a service or the furnishing of a product. The term information technology includes computers, ancillary equipment, software, firmware, and similar procedures, services (including support services), and related resources.
Information Technology Product	A system, component, application, etc., that is based upon technology which is used to electronically process, store, or transmit information.

Malicious Code [NIST SP 800-53]	Software or firmware intended to perform an unauthorized process that will have adverse impact on the confidentiality, integrity, or availability of an information system. A virus, worm, Trojan horse, or other code-based entity that infects a host. Spyware and some forms of adware are also examples of malicious code.
Malware	See Malicious Code.
Media [FIPS 200]	Physical devices or writing surfaces including, but not limited to, magnetic tapes, optical disks, magnetic disks, large-scale integration (LSI) memory chips, and printouts (but not including display media) onto which information is recorded, stored, or printed within an information system.
Media Library	Stores, protects, and controls all authorized versions of media CIs.
Misconfiguration	An incorrect or subobtimal configuration of an information system or system component that may lead to vulnerabilities.
Network-Based Intrusion Detection and Prevention System [SP 800-94]	An intrusion detection and prevention system that monitors network traffic for particular network segments or devices and analyzes the network and application protocol activity to identify and stop suspicious activity.
Open Checklist Interactive Language (OCIL)	SCAP language for expressing security checks that cannot be evaluated without some human interaction or feedback.
Open Vulnerability and Assessment Language (OVAL)	SCAP language for specifying low-level testing procedures used by checklists.
Organization [FIPS 200, Adapted]	An entity of any size, complexity, or positioning within an organizational structure (e.g., a federal agency or, as appropriate, any of its operational elements).
Remote Access [NIST SP 800-53]	Access to an organizational information system by a user (or an information system) communicating through an external, non-organization-controlled network (e.g., the Internet).
Risk Management [NIST SP 800-39]	The program and supporting processes to manage information security risk to organizational operations (including mission, functions, image, reputation), organizational assets, individuals, other organizations, and the Nation, and includes: (i) establishing the context for risk-related activities; (ii) assessing risk; (iii) responding to risk once determined; and (iv) monitoring risk over time.
Risk Executive (Function) [CNSSI 4009]	An individual or group within an organization that helps to ensure that: (i) security risk-related considerations for individual information systems, to include the authorization decisions for those systems, are viewed from an organization-wide perspective with regard to the overall strategic goals and objectives of the organization in carrying out its missions and business functions; and (ii) managing risk from individual information systems is consistent across the organization, reflects organizational risk tolerance, and is considered along with other organizational risks affecting mission/business success.

Safeguards [CNSSI-4009, Adapted]	Protective measures prescribed to meet the security objectives (i.e., confidentiality, integrity, and availability) specified for an information system. Safeguards may include security features, management controls, personnel security, and security of physical structures, areas, and devices. Synonymous with security controls and countermeasures.
Security Configuration Management (SecCM)	The management and control of configurations for an information system to enable security and facilitate the management of risk.
Security Content Automation Protocol (SCAP)	A protocol currently consisting of a suite of seven specifications[32] that standardize the format and nomenclature by which security software communicates information about software flaws and security configurations.
Security Controls [FIPS 199]	The management, operational, and technical controls (i.e., safeguards or countermeasures) prescribed for an information system to protect the confidentiality, integrity, and availability of the system and its information.
Security Impact Analysis [CNSSI-4009 adapted]	The analysis conducted by an organizational official to determine the extent to which a change to the information system has or may have affected the security posture of the system.
Security Information and Event Management (SIEM) Tool	Application that provides the ability to gather security data from information system components and present that data as actionable information via a single interface.
Security Posture [CNSSI-4009 adapted]	The security status of an enterprise's networks, information, and systems based on information security resources (e.g., people, hardware, software, policies) and capabilities in place to manage the defense of the enterprise and to react as the situation changes.
Senior Agency Information Security Officer [44 U.S.C., Sec. 3544]	Official responsible for carrying out the Chief Information Officer responsibilities under the Federal Information Security Management Act (FISMA) and serving as the Chief Information Officer's primary liaison to the agency's authorizing officials, information system owners, and information systems security officers. [Note 1: With respect to SecCM, a Senior Agency Information Security Officer is an individual that provides organization-wide procedures and/or templates for SecCM, manages or participates in the Configuration Control Board, and/or provides technical staff for security impact analyses. Note 2: Organizations subordinate to federal agencies may use the term *Senior Information Security Officer* or *Chief Information Security Officer* to denote individuals filling positions with similar responsibilities to Senior Agency Information Security Officers.]
Senior Information Security Officer	See Senior Agency Information Security Officer.
Spyware [CNSSI-4009]	Software that is secretly or surreptitiously installed into an information system to gather information on individuals or organizations without their knowledge; a type of malicious code.

[32] Additional SCAP specifications are expected to be added, check http://scap.nist.gov/ for updates.

System	See Information System.
System Security Plan [NIST SP 800-18]	Formal document that provides an overview of the security requirements for the information system and describes the security controls in place or planned for meeting those requirements.
Threat [CNSSI-4009]	Any circumstance or event with the potential to adversely impact organizational operations (including mission, functions, image, or reputation), organizational assets, individuals, other organizations, or the Nation through an information system via unauthorized access, destruction, disclosure, modification of information, and/or denial of service.
Threat Source [FIPS 200]	The intent and method targeted at the intentional exploitation of a vulnerability or a situation and method that may accidentally trigger a vulnerability. Synonymous with threat agent.
United States Government Configuration Baseline (USGCB)[33]	The United States Government Configuration Baseline (USGCB) provides security configuration baselines for Information Technology products widely deployed across the federal agencies. The USGCB baseline evolved from the federal Desktop Core Configuration mandate. The USGCB is a Federal government-wide initiative that provides guidance to agencies on what should be done to improve and maintain an effective configuration settings focusing primarily on security.
User	See Information System User
Vulnerability [CNSSI-4009, Adapted]	Weakness in an information system, system security procedures, internal controls, or implementation that could be exploited or triggered by a threat source.
Whitelist [SP 800-94, Adapted]	A list of discrete entities, such as hosts or applications that are known to be benign and are approved for use within an organization and/or information system.

---

[33] http://usgcb.nist.gov/

APPENDIX C

ACRONYMS

COMMON ABBREVIATIONS

ARF	Asset Reporting Format
AV	Antivirus
CCB	Configuration Control Board
CCE	Common Configuration Enumeration
CCSS	Common Configuration Scoring System
CD	Compact Disc
CI	Configuration Item
CIO	Chief Information Officer
CIS	Center for Internet Security
CM	Configuration Management
CMMI	Capability Maturity Model Integration
CNSS	Committee for National Security Systems
COTS	Commercial Off-the-Shelf
CPE	Common Platform Enumeration
CVE	Common Vulnerabilities and Exposures
CVSS	Common Vulnerability Scoring System
DISA	Defense Information Systems Agency
DNS	Domain Name System
DVD	Digital Video Disc
EPP	Endpoint Protection Platform
FDCC	Federal Desktop Core Configuration
FIPS	Federal Information Processing Standards
FISMA	Federal Information Security Management Act
IDPS	Intrusion Detection and Prevention System
IS	Information System
ISA	Information System Administrator
ISC	Information System Component
ISO	International Organization for Standardization
ISO	Information System Owner
ISSO	Information System Security Officer
ISSM	Information System Security Manager
ISU	Information System User
IT	Information Technology

ITIL	Information Technology Infrastructure Library
NetBIOS	Network Basic Input/Output System
NIST	National Institute of Standards and Technology
NISTIR	National Institute of Standards and Technology Interagency Report
NC	Non-component
NSA	National Security Agency
OCIL	Open Checklist Interactive Language
OMB	Office of Management and Budget
OVAL	Open Vulnerability and Assessment Language
SecCM	Security-Focused Configuration Management
SISO	Senior Information Security Officer
SCAP	Security Content Automation Program
SDLC	System Development Life Cycle
SSE-CMM	Systems Security Engineering - Capability Maturity Model®
SIEM	Security Information and Event Management
SLA	Service-Level Agreement
SP	Special Publication
SSH	Secure Shell
SSP	System Security Plan
STIG	Security Technical Implementation Guidelines
USB	Universal Serial Bus
US-CERT	United States Computer Emergency Readiness Team[34]
USGCB	United States Government Configuration Baseline
XML	Extensible Markup Language
XCCDF	Extensible Configuration Checklist Description Format

---

[34] http://www.us-cert.gov/

APPENDIX D

SAMPLE OUTLINE FOR A SECURITY CONFIGURATION MANAGEMENT PLAN

The following is an outline for developing a SecCM Plan for an organization and/or an information system. Organizations are encouraged to adapt the outline to make it suitable for their operational environment.

1. INTRODUCTION
    1.1 BACKGROUND *[Overview of SecCM and its purpose]*
    1.2 OVERVIEW OF SYSTEM *[System description; may reference relevant section of System Security Plan]*
        1.2.1 System Mission
        1.2.2 Data Flow Description
        1.2.3 System Architecture
        1.2.4 System Administration and Management Activities
    1.3 PURPOSE OF THIS DOCUMENT *[Use of this document]*
    1.4 SCOPE *[Applicability of this plan]*
    1.5 APPLICABLE POLICIES AND PROCEDURES
        [List of applicable federal and organizational policies, standards, and procedures]

2. SecCM PROGRAM
    2.1 SecCM ROLES AND RESPONSIBILITIES *[Description of roles/responsibilities for SecCM]*
    2.2 SecCM PROGRAM ADMINISTRATION *[Policies, Procedures, CCB]*
        2.2.1 SecCM Policies and Procedures (included herein or by reference)
        2.2.2 Configuration Control Board Functions
        2.2.3 Establishment of Change Control Board at the Organization Level
        2.2.4 Establishment of Change Control Board at the System Level
        2.2.5 Schedules and Resource Requirements
    2.3 SecCM TOOLS *[Tools and Archival locations for CCB]*
        2.3.1 SCM Tools
        2.3.2 SCM Library
    2.4 SecCM RETENTION, ARCHIVING, STORAGE AND DISPOSAL
        [Requirements for managing historical information on CIs, changes, etc.]

3. SecCM ACTIVITIES
    3.1 CONFIGURATION IDENTIFICATION
        3.1.1 Types of Configuration Items (CI) *[Description of categories of CIs, such as HW, Documentation, SW and scripts, Web pages]*
        3.1.2 Identification Criteria *[How to determine which Information System Components will be included with which CIs]*
        3.1.3 Configuration Item Labeling *[Naming convention for CIs]*
    3.2 CONFIGURATION BASELINING *[Defining the information to be included in baseline for each CI]*
        3.2.1 Identification of Applicable Common Secure Configurations
        3.2.2 Information System Component CI Baselines

3.2.3   Non-Component Object CI Baselines

3.3 CONFIGURATION CHANGE CONTROL   *[Requirements related to Configuration Change Control]*

3.3.1   Handling of Scheduled, Unscheduled, and Unauthorized Changes

3.3.2   Security Impact Analysis

3.3.3   Testing

3.3.4   Submission of Findings to the Change Control Board

3.3.5   Change Control Board Evaluation and Approval Process

3.3.6   Recording Requirements

3.4 SecCM MONITORING   *[Requirements related to monitoring baseline configurations and adherence to SecCM policies]*

3.4.1   Organization Level Tools

3.4.2   System Level Tools

3.4.3   Monitoring Requirements and Frequencies

3.5 SecCM REPORTING   *[Requirements related to reporting SecCM monitoring results and statistics to appropriate organizational staff]*

3.5.1   Report Recipients

3.5.2   Reviewing Reports

Suggested SecCM Plan APPENDICES:

CCB Charter

Change Request Form Template

Security Impact Analysis Report Format

References

APPENDIX E

SAMPLE CHANGE REQUEST
A TEMPLATE

The following is a sample template for a Change Request artifact that can be used within a SecCM program. Organizations are encouraged to adapt it to suit their needs.

1. **Date Prepared**:

2. **Title of Change Request**:

3. **Change Initiator/Project Manager**:

4. **Change Description**:

5. **Change Justification**:

6. **Urgency of Change**: {Scheduled/Urgent/Unscheduled}

7. **IS Components/CIs to be Changed**:

8. **Other IS Components, CIs, or Systems to Be Affected by Change**:

9. **Personnel involved with the Change**:

10. **Expected Security Impact of Change**:

11. **Expected Functional Impact of Change**:

12. **Expected Impact of Not Doing Change**:

13. **Potential Interface/Integration Issues**:

14. **Required Changes to Existing Applications**:

15. **Project work plan including change implementation date, deliverables, and back-out plan**:

16. **Funding Required to Implement Change**:

Change Approved/Disapproved (include justification and/or further action to be taken if disapproved):

Authorized Signature(s):

NOTE: Supporting documentation may be attached to the Change Request.

BEST PRACTICES FOR ESTABLISHING SECURE CONFIGURATIONS

Although there is no one-size-fits-all approach to SecCM, there are practices that organizations consider when developing and deploying secure configurations. These include:

1. Use Common Secure Configurations for Settings

Organizations consider available common secure configurations as the basis for establishing secure configuration settings. A comprehensive source for information on configuration settings is the National Checklist Program (http://checklists nist.gov). These checklists cover a wide range of commercial products and are written in a standardized format to facilitate automatic assessment through SCAP-enabled tools.

References:
NIST SP 800-27: *Engineering Principles for Information Technology Security (A Baseline for Achieving Security)*;
NIST SP 800-68: *Guide to Securing Microsoft Windows XP Systems for IT Professionals*;
NIST SP 800-69: *Guidance for Securing Microsoft Windows XP Home Edition: A NIST Security Configuration Checklist*;
NIST SP 800-70: *National Checklist Program for IT Products-Guidelines for Checklist Users and Developers*; and
NIST SP 800-117: *Guide to Adopting and Using the Security Content Automation Protocol (SCAP)*; and
http://nvd nist.gov.

2. Centralize Policy and Common Secure Configurations for Configuration Settings

Where possible and appropriate, secure configurations are developed and implemented in a top-down approach to ensure consistency across the organization. An example is the implementation of the group policy functionality, which can be used to distribute secure configuration policy in a centralized manner throughout established domains. Exceptions to the organization's policy may be needed to tailor configurations for a particular information system to support local constraints or requirements. Such exceptions are documented and approved as a part of the baseline configuration for that information system.

References: None.

3. Tailor Secure Configurations According to System/Component Function and Role

Secure configuration settings are tailored to the system component's function. For example, a server acting as a Windows domain controller may require stricter auditing requirements (e.g., auditing successful and unsuccessful account logons) than a file server. A public access Web server in a DMZ may require that fewer services are running than in a Web server behind an organization's firewall supporting an intranet.

References:
NIST SP 800-41: *Guidelines on Firewalls and Firewall Policy*;
NIST SP 800-44: *Guidelines on Securing Public Web Servers*;
NIST SP 800-45: *Guidelines on Electronic Mail Security*;
NIST SP 800-46: *Guide to Enterprise Telework and Remote Access Security*;

NIST SP 800-48: *Guide to Securing Legacy IEEE 802.11 Wireless Networks;*
NIST SP 800-52: *Guidelines for the Selection and Use of Transport Layer Security (TLS) Implementations;*
NIST SP 800-54: *Border Gateway Protocol Security;*
NIST SP 800-58: *Security Considerations for Voice Over IP Systems;*
NIST SP 800-77: *Guide to IPsec VPNs;*
NIST SP 800-81: *Secure Domain Name System (DNS) Deployment Guide;*
NIST SP 800-82: *Guide to Industrial Control Systems (ICS) Security;*
NIST SP 800-92: *Guide to Computer Security Log Management;*
NIST SP 800-95: *Guide to Secure Web Services;*
NIST SP 800-97: *Establishing Wireless Robust Security Networks: A Guide to IEEE 802.11i;*
NIST SP 800-98: *Guidelines for Securing Radio Frequency Identification (RFID) Systems;*
NIST SP 800-113: *Guide to SSL VPNs;*
NIST SP 800-121: *Guide to Bluetooth Security;*
NIST SP 800-123: *Guide to General Server Security;* and
NIST SP 800-124: *Guidelines on Cell Phone and PDA Security.*

4. Eliminate Unnecessary Ports, Services, and Protocols (Least Functionality)

Devices are configured to allow only the necessary ports, protocols, and services in accordance with functional needs and the risk tolerance in the organization. Open ports and available protocols and services are an inviting target for attackers, especially if there are known vulnerabilities associated with a given port, protocol, or service. Sources such as the NIST National Vulnerability Database (NVD) are available for highlighting vulnerabilities in various system components.

References: http://nvd.nist.gov/.

5. Limit the Use of Remote Connections

While connecting remotely to information systems allows more flexibility in how users and system administrators accomplish their work, it also opens an avenue of attack popular with hackers. Use of remote connections is limited to only those absolutely necessary for mission accomplishment.

References:
NIST SP 800-41: *Guidelines on Firewalls and Firewall Policy;*
NIST SP 800-46: *Guide to Enterprise Telework and Remote Access Security;*
NIST SP 800-47: *Security Guide for Interconnecting Information Technology Systems;*
NIST SP 800-52: *Guidelines for the Selection and Use of Transport Layer Security (TLS) Implementations;*
NIST SP 800-54: *Border Gateway Protocol Security;*
NIST SP 800-77: *Guide to IPsec VPNs;*
NIST SP 800-81: *Secure Domain Name System (DNS) Deployment Guide;*
NIST SP 800-95: *Guide to Secure Web Services;* and
NIST SP 800-113: *Guide to SSL VPNs.*

6. Develop Strong Password Policies

Passwords are a common mechanism for authenticating the identity of users and if they are poorly implemented or used, an attacker can undermine the best secure configuration. Organizations stipulate password policies and related requirements with the strength appropriate for protecting access to the organization's assets.

References:
NIST SP 800-63: *Electronic Authentication Guideline*;
NIST SP 800-118: *Guide to Enterprise Password Management* (Draft);
NIST SP 800-132: *Recommendation for Password-Based Key Derivation Part 1: Storage Applications*; and
NIST SP 800-135: *Recommendation for Existing Application-Specific Key Derivation Functions*.

7. Implement Endpoint Protection Platforms (EPPs)

Personal computers are a fundamental part of any organization's information system. They are an important source of connecting end users to networks and information systems, and are also a major source of vulnerabilities and a frequent target of attackers looking to penetrate a network. User behavior is difficult to control and hard to predict, and user actions, whether it is clicking on a link that executes malware or changing a security setting to improve the usability of their PC, frequently allow exploitation of vulnerabilities. Commercial vendors offer a variety of products to improve security at the "endpoints" of a network. These EPPs include:

a. Anti-malware

Anti-malware applications are part of the common secure configurations for system components. Anti-malware software employs a wide range of signatures and detection schemes, automatically updates signatures, disallows modification by users, run scans on a frequently scheduled basis, has an auto-protect feature set to scan automatically when a user action is performed (e.g., opening or copying a file), and may provide protection from zero-day attacks. For platforms for which anti-malware software is not available, other forms of anti-malware such as rootkit detectors may be employed.

b. Personal Firewalls

Personal firewalls provide a wide range of protection for host machines including restriction on ports and services, control against malicious programs executing on the host, control of removable devices such as USB devices, and auditing and logging capability.

c. Host-based Intrusion Detection and Prevention System (IDPS)

Host-based IDPS is an application that monitors the characteristics of a single host and the events occurring within that host to identify and stop suspicious activity. This is distinguished from network-based IDPS, which is an intrusion detection and prevention system that monitors network traffic for particular network segments or devices and analyzes the network and application protocol activity to identify and stop suspicious activity.

d. Restrict the use of mobile code

Organizations exercise caution in allowing the use of "mobile code" such as ActiveX, Java, and JavaScript. An attacker can easily attach a script to a URL in a Web page or email that, when clicked, will execute malicious code within the computer's browser.

References:
NIST SP 800-28: *Guidelines on Active Content and Mobile Code*;
NIST SP 800-41: *Guidelines on Firewalls and Firewall Policy*;
NIST SP 800-47: *Security Guide for Interconnecting Information Technology Systems*;
NIST SP 800-54: *Border Gateway Protocol Security*; and
NIST SP 800-94: *Guide to Intrusion Detection and Prevention Systems (IDPS)*.

8. Use Cryptography

In many systems, especially those processing, storing, or transmitting information that is moderate impact or higher for confidentiality, cryptography is considered as a part of an information system's secure configuration. There are a variety of places to implement cryptography to protect data including individual file encryption, full disk encryption, Virtual Private Network connections, etc.

References:
FIPS 140-2: *Security Requirements for Cryptography Modules*;
NIST SP 800-21: *Guideline for Implementing Cryptography in the Federal Government*;
NIST SP 800-25: *Federal Agency Use of Public Key Technology for Digital Signatures and Authentication*;
NIST SP 800-29: *A Comparison of the Security Requirements for Cryptographic Modules in FIPS 140-1 and FIPS 140-2*;
NIST SP 800-32: *Introduction to Public Key Technology and the Federal PKI Infrastructure*;
NIST SP 800-57 *(parts 1-3): Recommendation for Key Management*;
NIST SP 800-107: *Recommendation for Applications Using Approved Hash Algorithms*;
NIST SP 800-111: *Guide to Storage Encryption Technologies for End User Devices*;
NIST SP 800-130, *A Framework for Designing Cryptographic Key Management Systems*; and
NIST SP 800-131A, *Transitions: Recommendation for Transitioning the Use of Cryptographic Algorithms and Key Lengths*.

9. Develop a Patch Management Process

A robust patch management process is important in reducing vulnerabilities in an information system. As patches greatly impact the secure configuration of an information system, the patch management process is integrated into SecCM at a number of points within the four SecCM phases including:

- Performing security impact analysis of patches;
- Testing and approving patches as part of the configuration change control process;
- Updating baseline configurations to include current patch level;
- Assessing patches to ensure they were implemented properly; and
- Monitoring systems/components for current patch status.

References:
NIST SP 800-40: *Creating a Patch and Vulnerability Program.*

10. Control Software Installation

The installation of software is a point where many vulnerabilities are introduced into an organization's information system. Malware or insecure software can give attackers easy access to an organization's otherwise tightly protected network. Although the simplest approach is to lock down computers and manage software installation centrally (i.e., at the organizational level), this is not always a viable option for some organizations. Other methods for controlling the installation of software include:

- Whitelisting – All software is checked against a list approved by the organization;
- Checksums – All software is checked to make sure the code has not changed;
- Certificate – Only software with signed certificates from a trusted vendor is used;
- Path or domain – Only software within a directory or domain can be installed; and
- File extension – Software with certain file extensions such as .bat cannot be installed.

REFERENCES: NONE.

SᴇᴄCM PROCESS FLOW CHARTS

The following flow charts provide examples of the SecCM phases and SecCM activities for those phases that could be considered in developing SecCM processes. Organizations are encouraged to adapt the flow charts to make it suitable for them operating environment.

Security-Focused Configuration Management Phases

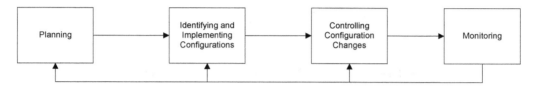

Organizational-Level Security-Focused Configuration Management Program
Planning Step Tasks
(Section 3.1.1)

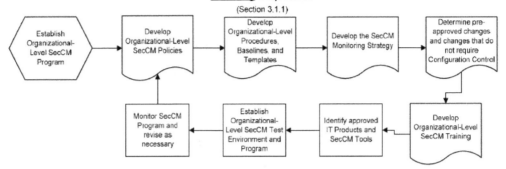

System-Level Security-Focused Configuration Management Program Planning
Step Tasks
(Section 3.1.2)

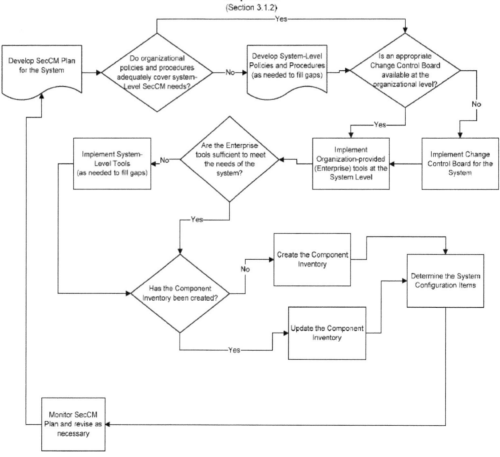

System-Level Security-Focused Configuration Management
<u>Identifying and Implementing Configurations</u> Step Tasks
(Section 3.2)

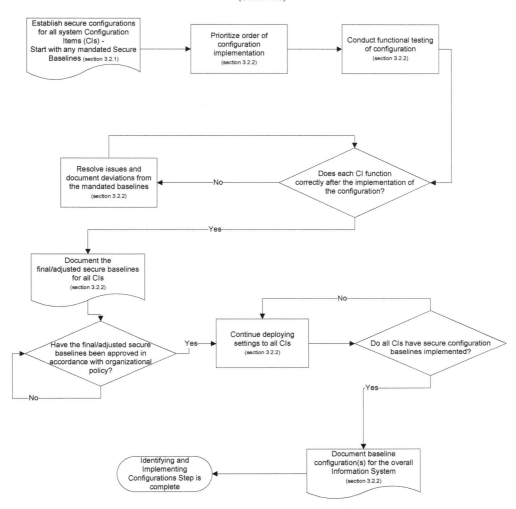

System-Level Security-Focused Configuration Management
<u>Controlling Configuration Changes</u> Step Tasks
(Section 3.3)

Controlling Configuration Change – <u>Implement Configuration Change Control Process</u>
(Section 3 3 2)

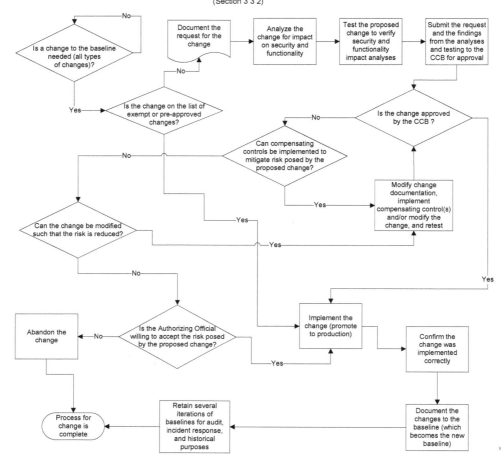

Controlling Configuration Changes – <u>Conduct Security Impact Analyses</u>
(Section 3.3.3)

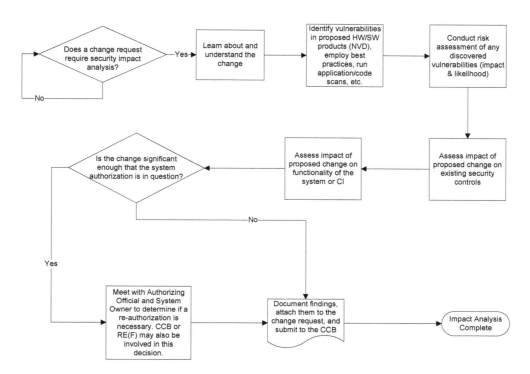

Organizational-Level Security-Focused Configuration Management Program <u>Monitoring</u> Step

Implement the SecCM Monitoring Strategy and Schedule
(Section 3.4)

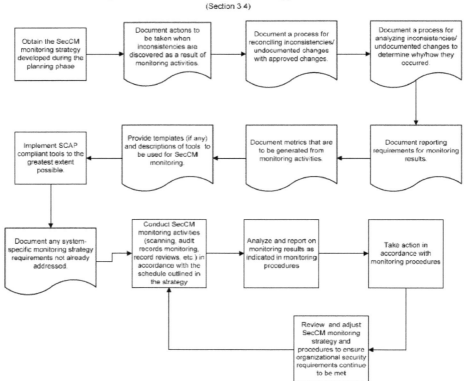

CCB CHARTER SAMPLE

The following is a sample template for a CCB charter that can be used within a SecCM program. Organizations are encouraged to adapt it to suit their needs.

Configuration Control Board Charter

PURPOSE

<Describe the objectives of the CCB. It might say something like:"The Configuration Control Board (CCB) represents the interests of program and project management by ensuring that a structured process is used to consider proposed changes and incorporate them into a specified release of a product. The CCB shall request that impact analysis of proposed changes be performed, review change requests, make decisions, and communicate decisions made to affected groups and individuals." Define the relationship of this CCB to any other CCBs in the organization or other decision-making bodies, such as a project steering committee.>

SCOPE OF AUTHORITY

<Indicate the scope of decisions that the CCB makes. This scope could be over a specific organizational range; a project, group of projects (program), or subproject; a maximum budget or schedule impact. This scope boundary separates decisions that this CCB can make from those that it must escalate to a higher-level CCB or manager for resolution.>

MEMBERSHIP

<List the members of this CCB. The CCB typically includes representatives from program management, project management, software engineering, hardware engineering, testing, documentation, customer support, and marketing. One individual is designated as the CCB Chair. Keep the CCB as small as possible, to facilitate its ability to make rapid decisions, but make sure that the critical perspectives are represented.>

OPERATING PROCEDURES

<State the frequency of regularly scheduled CCB meetings and the conditions that will trigger a special meeting. Describe how meetings will be conducted, the number of CCB members who constitute a quorum to make decisions at a meeting, and the roles that must be represented for the meeting to proceed. Identify whether guest participants may attend, such as the individuals who proposed the change requests being considered at a specific meeting.>

DECISION-MAKING PROCESS

<Describe how the CCB will make its decisions. Indicate whether voting, consensus, unanimity, delegation to a specific individual, or some other decision rule is used to make decisions. State whether the CCB Chair or another manager is permitted to overrule the CCB's collective decision.>

COMMUNICATING STATUS

<Describe how each decision that the CCB makes will be communicated to the individual who requested the change, senior management, project management, affected team members who must implement the change, higher- or lower-level CCBs, and any other stakeholders. Indicate where the decisions and any supporting information, rationale, or data will be stored.>

SAMPLE SECURITY IMPACT ANALYSIS TEMPLATE

The following is a sample template for a Security Impact Analysis that can be used within a SecCM program. Organizations are encouraged to adapt it to suit their needs.

The [*insert relevant parties, e.g., Change Control Board, Information system Owner (ISO), Information System Security Officer (ISSO),system administrators, security assessors*] complete Tables 1-6, which will be used to review the change and determine requirements.

Table 1: Initiative/Release Background

[TEMPLATE NOTE: Pre-filled information in Table 1 is for illustrative purposes only and should be replaced with information applicable to individual organizations]

Initiative/Release Name	
Project Type	[Examples only]: **-New Development:** *[insert description]* **-Enhancement**: *[insert description]* **-Maintenance**: *[insert description]* *[Insert project types and descriptions as applicable]*
System Changes	**Provide an overview of the changes.**
Baseline Changes	**Provide description of the new baseline.**
Security Risks	**Provide any risks or impacts on the system.**
Planned Deployment Initiation Date	
Planned Deployment Completion Date	
System(s) Impacted by change	
Current Security Categorization of Impacted System(s)	
[Insert initiative/release background info required by the organization as applicable]	

Table 2: Initiative/Release Description and Potential Security Issues
[TEMPLATE NOTE: Pre-filled information in Table 2 is for illustrative purposes only and should be replaced with information applicable to individual organizations]

What are the business requirements driving the change?
Please provide a description of the proposed change(s), including ALL additions, deletions, and modifications.
Is the Technical Lead and/or Project Lead aware of any potential security-related issues or challenges associated with this change? If so, briefly describe them or provide and attachment describing them.

Table 3: Change Type Worksheet

Please review the list of Change Types below. In the second column, mark each applicable change type with an "X". Provide a brief explanation of why applicable change types are selected in the third column. The change types are not intended to be mutually exclusive, so multiple change types may be selected for a single initiative/release. If none of the change types are applicable, please mark "Other change" and provide a description of the change in the third column.

[TEMPLATE NOTE: Change type provided in Table 3 are for illustrative purposes only and should be replaced with changes types applicable to individual organizations]

Change Type	Applicable? (Mark X if Applicable)	Explanation (If Applicable)
New network device(s) (e.g., router, switch, firewall, VPN gateway)		
New server(s)		
New workstation(s) (desktops or laptops)		
Other new HW		
Decommissioning of existing HW		
New virtual server		
New OS		
Upgrade of existing OS		
New COTS application		
Upgrade or patch of COTS application		
New custom application		
Upgrade or bug fix for existing custom application		
New DBMS (e.g., Microsoft SQL Server or Oracle)		
Upgrade of existing DBMS (e.g., Oracle		

Change Type	Applicable? (Mark X if Applicable)	Explanation (If Applicable)
9i to 10g)		
Addition of new DB instance		
Modification of an existing DB instance (e.g., changes to a table)		
New or upgraded Middleware application or service		
Modifications to ports, protocols, and services used or provided by the system		
Changes intended to address security requirements or improve/modify the security of the system (e.g., cryptographic modules, security patch, authentication, authorization, role changes)		
New information type processed, stored, or transmitted on the system		
Interface change (addition/removed)		
Change of location		
Other change		

Table 4: Device Impact Worksheet

[TEMPLATE NOTE: Column headings in Table 4 are for illustrative purposes only and should be replaced with information relevant/applicable to individual organizations]

System Name	Device Name	IP Address	Manufacturer Model	Serial No.	Asset/ Component Property ID	OS	Software	Description

Table 5: Testing Worksheet

[TEMPLATE NOTE: Pre-filled information in Table 5 is for illustrative purposes only and should be replaced with information applicable to individual organizations]

Please describe the tests that were conducted against the change?

Please provide a description of the test results for each change (or provide reference to another document with test results).

Table 6: Analysis Worksheet
[TEMPLATE NOTE: Pre-filled information in Table 6 is for illustrative purposes only and should be replaced with information applicable to individual organizations]

Analysis, Recommendations, and Requirements
[Reviewed by: Name (Title)]

Signature

_____   _____

[*Insert relevant role*]   [Date]

Signature

_____   _____

[*Insert relevant role*]   [Date]

Signature

_____   _____

[*Insert relevant role*]   [Date]

ATTACHMENT 1
SECURITY IMPACT WORKSHEET

1. AC: Will change(s) to system effect how the system limits: (i) information system access to authorized users, processes acting on behalf of authorized users or devices (including other information systems); and (ii) the types of transactions and functions that authorized users are permitted to exercise.
If so, describe.

2. AT: Will change(s) affect required system training to ensure that personnel are adequately trained to carry out their assigned information security-related duties and responsibilities?
If so, describe.

3. AU: Will change(s) affect how system audit requirements to (i) create, protect, and retain information system audit records to the extent needed to enable the monitoring, analysis, investigation, and reporting of unlawful, unauthorized, or inappropriate information system activity; and (ii) ensure that the actions of individual information system users can be uniquely traced to those users so they can be held accountable for their actions.
If so, describe.

4. CM: Will change(s) to the system impact the (i) baseline configuration and inventory of organizational information systems; (ii) establishment and enforcement of security configuration settings; and (iii) ability to monitor and control changes to the baseline configurations and to the constituent components of the systems (including hardware, software, firmware, and documentation) throughout the respective system development life cycle.
If so, describe.

5. IA: Will change(s) to the system impact how it (i) identifies users, processes acting on behalf of users, or devices; and (ii) authenticates (or verifies) the identities of those users, processes, or devices, as a prerequisite to allowing access to organizational information systems.
If so, describe.

6. MA: Will change(s) to the system impact how (i) periodic and timely maintenance is performed; and (ii) provide effective controls on the tools, techniques, mechanisms, and personnel used to conduct information system maintenance.
If so, describe.

7. MP: Will change(s) to the system impact how (i) information contained in the systems in printed form or on digital media is protected; (ii) access to information in printed form or on digital media removed from the systems is limited to authorized users; and (iii) how digital media is sanitized or destroyed before disposal or release for reuse.
If so, describe.

8. PE: Will change(s) to the system/system environment change how (i) physical access to information systems, equipment, and the respective operating environments is limited

to authorized individuals; (ii) the physical plant and support infrastructure for information systems is protected; (iii) supporting utilities for information systems is provided; (iv) and (v) appropriate environmental controls in facilities are provided.
<u>If so, describe.</u>

9. SC: Will change(s) to the system effect how: (i) communications (i.e., information transmitted or received by organizational information systems) are monitored, controlled, and protected at the external boundaries and key internal boundaries of the information systems; and (ii) architectural designs, software development techniques, and systems engineering principles that promote effective information security are implemented.
<u>If so, describe.</u>

10. SI: Will change(s) to the system effect how (i) system flaws are identified, reported, and corrected in a timely manner; (ii) malicious code protection is employed; (iii) system events are monitored and detected; (iv) the correct operation of security functions is verified; and (v) information is checked for accuracy, completeness, validity, and authenticity.
<u>If so, describe.</u>